The Common Golfer

CELEBRATING THE GAME'S ORDINARY AND EXTRAORDINARY
PEOPLE, PLACES AND THINGS.

The Common Golfer

CELEBRATING THE GAME'S ORDINARY AND EXTRAORDINARY PEOPLE, PLACES AND THINGS.

Jack Wollitz

TUCKER DS PRESS

Cover & inside photos by Jack Wollitz
Cover design by Lee-Ann Mitchell DeMeo
Sunrise on the first tee is one of the wonders of golf. Every day's dawn is special in so many ways. Sunrise tee times are made better with four friends admiring the perfect start to a great day of golf. The photo was shot at Yankee Run Golf Course, Brookfield, Ohio. The cover was designed by the gifted artist Lee-Ann DeMeo.

Edited by David Bushman
Book designed by Scott Ryan

Published in the USA by Fayetteville Mafia/Tucker DS Press
Columbus, Ohio

Contact Information
Email: fayettevillemafiapress@gmail.com
Website: TuckerDSPress.com

DEDICATION

I am fortunate to have the best golf friends in the world. You know who you are. This book is dedicated to you and all the others.

Most of all The Common Golfer is dedicated to my wife, Barb, the better golfer of us two, and the lady who took my hand and led me to the first tee one fine spring day in 1976 and then a week later took my hand at the altar and said "I do." She's a birdie, for sure.

For me and for many, golf is a family matter. I must thank daughter Betsy and her husband, Irfan, for joining Barb and me whenever possible for some of the best rounds of golf ever. It has been an incomparable experience to witness Betsy take to the game when she was a young girl and now share her love of the game with Irfan. Speaking of family, I carry a 4-hybrid I claimed just a few months ago from the set Dad bought new at age ninety-one.

Finally, I certainly owe a huge thank-you to Don Woods, Barb's father, who instilled in her the love of golf and who, with Barb's mom, chaperoned us on a high school date at the World Series of Golf at Firestone Country Club in Akron, Ohio. Ray Floyd won, by the way.

CONTENTS

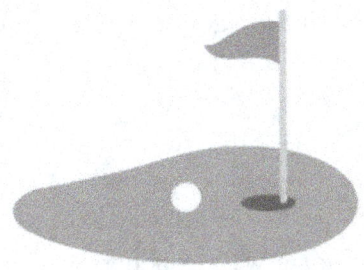

Introduction

Tiny drops of water flipped off the toes of my shoes as I walked to the golf ball that had settled a few feet from the freshly mowed fairway. The ball rested low in the grass. It was hittable. But the shot would be difficult—and difficult it proved to be. I took my stance, addressed the ball, waggled my club, and went through the checklist the club pro had recommended at the conclusion of my most recent lesson.

The morning was perfect for golf. My foursome were dew sweepers. First off the tee that day, we were enjoying fairways free of cart tracks and greens unmolested by footprints. The sun was starting to evaporate the water condensed on the blades of grass, but enough lingered to wet our shoes. Clumps of clippings from the predawn mower were scattered here and there along my trek across the fairway.

I arrived at the ball, happy to see it had not settled too deeply into its resting place in the rough. I also noticed the green grass glued by the dew to the toe of my FootJoy. My brain immediately forgot everything it knew about hitting golf balls. I wandered off to a place where the grass is dry, every lie is exquisite, and the strikes are swift and square. It was a nice place. My shoes were clean there.

Forget that clump, I scolded myself. *Focus. You've got this. Just hit the freakin' ball.* But that confounding clump of clippings screamed in the middle of my backswing, and the echo reverberated as the clubhead descended toward the waiting golf ball. The strike was imperfect—very imperfect in fact—and the ball squirted thirty feet left.

Another failed golf shot, yes. But we golfers have a superbly unique perspective about failures. A golfer I met summed up an attitude I

recommend for all of us common golfers. He celebrated all of his shots—
the good and the bad—with this thought:

It's closer to the hole and I can find it.

Indeed. Golf, I believe, is a game for the optimist in each of us.

• • •

Something about golf finds a way to penetrate the souls of millions of
people. Not just today, but over the span of centuries, people have picked
up sticks and swatted balls around lawns and beaches, fields and forests,
hardscrabble "cow pastures," and exquisitely manicured fairways and
greens. Golfers today gather from seacoasts to mountain meadows to see
whether they can hit their balls into four-and-a-quarter-inch-diameter
cups sunk in greens as smooth as a pool table.

That they are (and were) golfing is their common denominator.
Golfers are as diverse as our planet's population. Athletic and not so
much, obese and fit, tall and short. Most have two arms and two legs,
but some do not. Most can see, but some are blind. Some can laugh away
failed shots, but most cannot.

What thrills golfers about the experience is as personal as anything our
world offers. Golf is a challenge. It can be a competition. It is something
to do outdoors under a blazing sun or in places where snow is falling
from a gray sky in subfreezing temperatures.

Golf can cost ten dollars a round or a thousand dollars. You pay your
money and you take your hacks to gain the benefit—whatever it might
be—that inspired you to go to the golf course in the first place.

• • •

Recently my wife, Barb, and I were in the gallery at a professional golf
tournament. It was not our first time at a major sporting event. We've
been spectators at Major League Baseball, National Football League,
and National Basketball Association games. We've roamed the pits and
joined hundreds of thousands of people at the Indianapolis 500. We've
witnessed Formula One grand prix races. Each event has its special
following of zealous fans, party animals, and even hecklers—all of them
ready, willing, and able to express their appreciation and even disdain for
the performance of the competitors.

But professional golf tournaments are different. The people who go to watch them can witness only a fraction of the action at any given moment. They generally are well-behaved, reverent even. They cheer good shots, but for the most part they show their appreciation with polite applause—even for the pro who has finally tapped in a double-bogey putt. Some heckling is tolerated, but anything over-the-top is likely to get the offender escorted from the golf course.

American sportswriter Rick Reilly wrote a book entitled *Missing Links* that tells the fictional tale of a circle of friends who golf regularly at a tired old muni course just beyond the walls of a luxurious country club outside Boston. The friends are weary of their mundane experiences at their bedraggled track and soon cook up a competition to award one thousand dollars to the first of them to play a round at the esteemed and swanky New England country club next door. It is an entertaining story that underscores the great value of the little things in our lives that add up to form the foundation of what makes each of us unique, complete, and satisfied.

As I listened to people around me in the gallery at the pro golf tournament, I thought back to Reilly's Missing Links and how, as I read it, I recognized people with whom I've played golf. It occurred to me that the individuals around me—whether they played at their local muni or the most exclusive club in town—felt the same kinship with golf as the other men and women around us. I could literally hear that kinship from the words and terms they used and the reverence in the tone of their voices. They said the same things—right or wrong, truth or myth—that I hear during any of the three or four rounds I play each week year-round.

They were much like me even though we hailed from a hundred different places and worked in a wide variety of jobs. The people in the gallery almost certainly represented each and every rung on the ladder of social status and privilege. But while affluence and status might be good to get you into a prestigious golf club, they do nothing whatsoever to differentiate us from the people who save a portion of their paycheck so they can afford a round at the public golf course near home.

We are, I concluded, common golfers with an uncommon passion for the great game and true believers that regardless of what has transpired up to this point in our round, the next shot we are about to hit may very well be the best we've ever struck.

Golf is a lot like fishing in one particular way. The next cast or the next shot is an opportunity for great success. Golfers and anglers are optimists at heart. We share a bunch of other personality traits and quirks, but optimism is the one that pushes us to the lake and to the first tee. I wrote a book titled *The Common Angler* in celebration of the passion shared by people who fish.

This book is for and about the common golfer. The stories that follow are true, and the opinions expressed are mine. You may agree or disagree, but I believe you will recognize bits and pieces of yourself and your experiences in the people and events herein.

We are golfers, after all, people whose sport is about hitting and chasing a little white ball, finding it and then hitting it again. When it's all said and done, golf is about progress—on many levels as varied and personal as the individuals who swing the clubs.

So let's progress. Please turn the page and allow me to share my take on the game and the people who play it.

Jack Wollitz
December 2025

CHAPTER 1

Why do we golf?

Mark Twain once described golf as a good walk spoiled. He was a wise man, but I respectfully disagree with his quip about the game I have grown to love. I understand he was making an analogy about golf's frustrations. Nevertheless, I disagree.

Something about golf finds a way to penetrate the souls of millions of people. That we are golfing is our common denominator. But what thrills us about the experience is as personal as anything our world offers.

Golf is frustrating, but also rewarding. Golf is difficult, but almost anybody can play. Golf is tedious, but exciting. Golf may be inexpensive for one and costly for another. Golf is whatever you want it to be, but a little bit different for everybody.

The game is physical, but also a test for the mind. It's for the clearheaded and the emotional wrecks. Some of the greatest players have been among the fittest of athletes, but many champs have been chubby smokers. Golf is always a test, but rarely truly aced.

So why do we golf? Our why is impossible to define. To arrive at a universal "why" would be a marketing miracle, the answer to every executive whose career mission is to continually develop and sell to the population of golfers tools and gadgets they believe will take them to the next level in their most basic stick-and-ball sport.

Your why might be similar to my why. But who really knows? I can't tell you why you are passionate about golf. I cannot even tell you my own why.

I do believe the unsolvable riddle of golf's why is itself the reason the game has such a firm grip on its players.

On the surface, golf would seem to be a simple game. You hit a ball repeatedly until it drops into the hole. Along the way, you are expected to follow a few rules—and even penalize yourself if you break them. So that makes golf a game of eye-hand coordination and honesty.

But wait, there's more.

The ball to be struck is motionless on the ground, but the golfer's club must strike the ball as close as possible to the sweet spot of the club face. Success depends on the swinger's ability to coordinate their hands, arms, hips, legs, and feet and the most important body part in the game, the brain. The ball is motionless, but there are a thousand moving parts to be tuned and timed.

Say the golfer brings Baryshnikov grace to the course. Even then, more variables loom large. What is the variety of grass? How tall are the blades? What direction is the grain? Is the soil sand, clay, loam, or a mixture of each? Is it wet or dry? Is there wind? What direction is it

Every golf shot is a new opportunity to succeed. .

blowing? What club should they select for the shot? Lay up or go for it? How tall are those trees? Aim for the pin or shoot for the middle of the green? Does my shirt match my pants? Does this skort make my butt look big? Should I apply more sunscreen? Is my stance too wide? Is it too narrow? Will that putt break left? Leave the flag in or take it out? Why is that clump of grass on my shoe?

I could go on, but you get the picture. Golf is a game that gets in your head. You love it, yes, but you also deal with distractions that can come from literally anywhere, including, of course, those generated by electrical impulses deep in our brains.

So to Mark Twain I say this: golf is a good walk on a path where new opportunities come along every few minutes and where anything is possible.

The best I can define the "why" of my golf is that it scratches my itch for competition and proves satisfying just often enough to lure me back to the first tee time and again. I do not believe my mind will ever dismiss golf from my life, and I hope my body will remain able to keep me walking that path to the opportunities I know are just one more swing from becoming reality.

Golf is frustrating yet rewarding,
physical but also a test for the mind.

CHAPTER 2

Is it work or is it fun?

Let me begin by saying golf, in my book, is not work. I've been to work, and based on my on-the-job experience spanning more than fifty years, I can affirm that golf is not work.

Golf is fun.

Some would disagree. They would say golfers must work to succeed in golf; therefore golf is work. I say, however, that before golfers decide to work on their games, they first must determine the game itself is fun.

In life and in living, fun is where we find it. It can be at a carnival or a ball game, a forest trail or a snow-covered ski slope, a mountain stream or a surf-crashed beach, a good book or a three-star restaurant.

Golfers find fun on green lawns pocked by small holes in eighteen different locations. Here I digress for a moment to differentiate between work and effort, because to succeed in golf requires effort that should be fun. If your efforts to achieve greater success in golf are drudgery, then you will not continue to invest the time and money to get to where you wish to be.

So, yes, golf is fun. At its best, golf is a progression of moments over the course of four hours that makes us smile and laugh, that elevates our hopes and rewards our efforts. Even at its worst, golfing is a pastime far better than all but a half dozen other life situations.

Interestingly, what one golfer finds as fun, another might not. Certainly, however, great fun includes well-struck shots, the pleasure of good company, a silky-smooth fairway, a pristine green, the celebration of success, and the rollicking nineteenth hole (timed to arrive, says legend and lore, just as the ancient golfer's flask ran dry).

Looking back across many decades of golf, I see a panorama of people and places playing through in fun fashion.

I see my thrill at deciphering the riddle daughter Betsy and son-in-law Irfan conjured up to announce their gift as Barb and I headed into retirement. Spoiler alert: it was a trip to Pebble Beach, Spyglass, and the Inn at Spanish Bay. Wow!

The fun times include my first ace—as well as the second, third, fourth, and fifth. The joy was over-the-top, but I was just as joyful when I witnessed two of Barb's aces and those of a half-dozen friends whose tee shots found the bottoms of cups.

Golf can be fun played solo, but count me in the crowd of those who believe golf is best enjoyed with friends. For that reason, I joined an after-work golf league and wangled an invitation to a Sunday grasshopper gang. Great fun and a million memories, for sure.

Fun is where you find it, and Barb and I find fun aplenty with the members of our club in Naples, Florida. We always have a lot of laughs, high fives, and birdie juice with those who make up our foursomes.

Workday golf is great fun too. I learned this at age seventeen when the owner of the gas station where I worked told me to tuck in my shirt and accompany him to the golf course for a quick nine. Really. Those rounds were way more fun than changing oil and answering the bell that announced cars needing fuel at twentieth century service stations.

Years later, with a white collar job paying my salary, workday golf was an occasional treat, fun breaks from the eight-to-five toils for our clients. Fun, yes, but with great respect for their fun at our expense.

Fun is the hour spent rocking on the porch of the clubhouse beyond the iconic eighteenth hole at Pinehurst, especially with a cold drink to sip while watching golfers and caddies wrapping up their four hours of fun.

I'm an explorer by nature, always wondering what's up around the bend. So you can appreciate the fun I feel driving up the lane of a club I'm visiting for the first (or umpteenth) time and the view of the clubhouse looking back from the first tee.

Getting new stuff is all part of the fun. A new driver, a set of irons, or a fine-tuned putter is a fun extension of our connection to the game, but so are opening a new sleeve of golf balls, stocking a new bag, and tugging on a perfectly fitted new glove.

I could go on, as I'm certain you can too, because golf is never the same, no matter how often we play. The fun doesn't have to stop—and in fact, it never does. No two days are ever equal, and the promise is that even if today is the most fun you've ever experienced, tomorrow is likely to be even better.

Even when the world seems to be on
fire, golf is our retreat to fun.

CHAPTER 3

A first time for everyone

Most people remember their first. Or at least they have fuzzy recollections of the situation and the person with whom they shared the experience. For me, it was outdoors, behind the house on a hot and humid summer afternoon. Our neighborhood kids often gathered at someone's home and did what kids do to while away the lazy days of summer. Soon enough we became teens and felt the urge to try new stuff, to test the limits of our flowing hormones and growing strength, and to seek conquests in new and exciting dimensions. It was the 1960s and everybody seemed to be experimenting, so what the heck, let's go for it. If we're careful, we reasoned, nobody would get hurt.

Hey, we're talking golf here. The first time I hit a golf ball was in the backyard of my parents' home. Dad was at work. Mom was tending to baby sister. Our suburban lot extended more than one hundred yards behind the house, lots of space for a twelve-year-old to hit a golf ball gleaned from Dad's bag leaning in a corner of the garage with a club plucked from the same bag. I never asked for permission, calculating the odds favored a denial, so we grabbed our stuff, snuck out behind the house, and took a swing at another of life's great thrills.

Making flush contact with a speeding clubface against a solid golf ball is an incomparable experience.

To the neophyte, golf would seem to be a simple endeavor. Indeed,

I once worked for a nongolfer who scoffed that while golf might be a game, it did not require much in terms of athleticism. He reasoned that the fat guys he saw on televised matches seemed to be as capable of winning as the trim golfers. He had never tried the game, but he opined that rolling a golf ball into a hole was a matter of luck rather than skill. And, he declared, hitting a 100 mph round baseball with a rounded bat was a feat of substance compared with swatting a small ball resting stationary on solid ground. Obviously, the boss had no clue about the torturous approach we golfers practice in our search for success.

My first attempts to hit golf shots are long forgotten. Whiffs? I'm sure there were many. Slices? Indeed! Hooks? I would say so. Worm burners? Oh, I'd bet the ranch on that.

What I do know is that sometime early on, I must have made contact pure enough to be utterly satisfying. I say this with certainty because had those moments of pleasure not happened early, I would more than likely have set the clubs aside and stuck with riding my bicycle and fishing in the creek in the woods beyond the house.

My backyard was big enough for preteen boys to compete. Dad had planted several maple and tulip trees as well as a peach tree that served as the final hole on the course. We aimed tee shots at tree trunks and chipped until our ball knocked on the wood. Our score was the number of times we hit the ball. As we boys gained strength and skill, we changed to hollow plastic balls to minimize the chances of denting siding and breaking windows. The peegee balls actually helped us expand our golf course, as we could hit over the house to trees in the front yard.

What joy we had, so much satisfaction, and as comes with this game, so many frustrations.

In the weeks and months that ensued after our first time, we made rapid progress in the game. We learned about hooking, slicing, chunking, and the yips. We also learned big lessons about life and living. We learned about honor, integrity, and cheating, and striving, practicing and achieving.

Golf, at least our boyhood version, was an important part of growing up in the neighborhood of my youth.

CHAPTER 4

The game goes forward

Among the many things that distinguish golf from other sports is the fact that play always moves forward.

In soccer, the ball is kicked left or right, forward or backward, depending on the goal that is your target. Basketball is similar. Players dribble and pass, from left to right or right to left "across your radio dial," as legendary play-by-play man Joe Tait explained to listeners of radio broadcasts of the NBA's Cleveland Cavaliers.

Football teams hope to move the pigskin to their foes' goals but do sometimes suffer setbacks resulting in the ball moving away from the end zone. Baseball? The ball comes in and goes out. It is pitched, thrown, batted, and bunted. The ball is allowed to bound on the ground, fly high, and travel far. A good outcome can result from a ball batted four feet forward or four hundred, and the score accumulates based on players advancing without being in possession of the ball. Thank you, Alexander Joy Cartwright.

But golf is different. It is a game of perpetual forward motion. The player should always be hitting the golf ball away from his or her position on the course toward the flag in the hole ahead.

For this reason, and for several others, I see golf as a game of positive momentum. No shot is a complete failure as long as it comes to rest closer to the hole than it was when you struck it.

But wait a moment, you say, what about those shots that do land

Unlike baseballs, soccer balls, and tennis balls, the golf ball is supposed to go only forward

behind the golfer? There are only two proper explanations. One is accidental; the other is on purpose.

Remember above I wrote "the player should always be hitting the golf ball . . . toward the flag"? The verb "should" is operative. Sometimes the player should not try a forward shot. A ball behind a tree, for example, might be best played *away* from the hole. In that case, the player can only go forward by first going backward. Isn't golf weird?

Speaking of weird, let's consider the other golf shots that might end up behind the golfer. They are the accidental shots that carom off a rock, tree, fence, golf cart, or whatever else might be in the line between the ball and the forward target.

In baseball, basketball, soccer, and football (as well as tennis, ping pong, volleyball, and every other ball sport), the field of play is clearly defined, with areas declared as either fair or foul or out-of-bounds. Any ball not out-of-bounds is generally considered to be in play.

In golf, of course, we have different rules for what we can do with the ball depending on where it lies in the field of play. Balls landing out-of-bounds must be replayed from their original position with the addition of a penalty stroke. But other landing spots have their own special circumstances. Balls on the fairway cannot be touched by anything other than players' clubs. Balls on greens can be marked, lifted, and cleaned. Players must not ground their clubs in certain penalty areas, such as sand traps, but recent rule changes permit grounding in other so-called penalty areas.

Consider that in baseball, players score without possession of the ball. In football, the ball itself scores, but not always in the possession of a player (and not necessarily in the possession of a player on the team that gets the points). It gets complicated in basketball too, because a ball passing through the hoop may earn the team one, two, or three points.

Is your head spinning?

Despite a thick rule book and playing venues too numerous to count and too diverse to categorize, golf really is a simple game with a simple strategy for moving a stationary ball toward a stationary target.

It is about forward progress, regardless of the circumstances. It is about forgetting the past and anticipating the best possible outcome. It is about aspiration, optimism, concentration, and motivation.

We hit the ball forward, find it, and hit it again.

CHAPTER 5

Your best golf buddies

One of the beautiful elements of golf is the people with whom we share our four hours of fun. As tee time approaches, we gather at the carts and ready our equipment, chattering about everything and nothing as we wind up our muscles and brains for the game that is about to begin. Regardless of the outcome, the round will be better because of the people around us.

I do believe that. The people with whom I have played are among my best friends. It's not surprising. We share the common denominator: love of golf.

Today, I have two corps of golf friends, one in Ohio and one Florida. The Ohio gang includes Ralph Roberts, Jim Zarlenga, Stan Czeck, Jack Savage, Mike Malito, Bob Catcott, Paul Pirko, and several others depending on who can play on any given day. We ante up eleven dollars and battle through eighteen holes for team honors, greenies, low net, and skins. Nobody goes broke, but nobody gets rich either.

The Florida boys include the dozen regulars who tee up every Monday in team better ball matches. We hail from Massachusetts, Illinois, North Carolina, Wisconsin, and New York. I'm the sole Ohioan. Snowbirds all, our regular group includes our "commissioner," Mike Kreeger, Tim Leary, Dave Tenaglia, Paul Parrone, Jimmy Duggan, Jim MacDonald, Dan Blanch, Glenn Gallant, Dave Newcomb, Bob Brown, Bob Guido, and yours truly. We are fortunate to have alternates ready to step in on any given Monday: Fred Suman, Don Nicholas, Mark Ondrako, Rick

McGinn, and John Horgan.

Our group is tight-knit. We declare often to each other that our Monday matches are our favorite rounds of the week, our seven-dollar entry paying huge dividends even when we lose. The ultimate prize is a red plastic belt, the buckle of which proudly declares its wearer as last season's champion. The belt is in my possession as I write this, but that's a story for another day.

Of course, there are hundreds of others who've joined me out there. If you're a golfer, you know these people:

Rich, Ted, Zar, Ralph, Stan, Jack, Mike, Cosmo, Doc, Mark, Glenn, Dave, Leo, Janet, Sally, Ann, Tom, Barb, Betsy, Irfan, Marianne, Mary, Deb, Joyce, Cindy, Patty, Paul, Paula, Pauline, Judy, Cindy, Nancy, Chris, Bruce, Tim, Rick, Bill, Bucky, Wayne, Jim, Jimmy, Kevin, Floyd, Duffy, Joe, Keith, Norm, Brian, Dan, Don, Carol, Dennis, Bob, Randy, Pierre, Angelo, Anthony, Sylvia, Lynn, Esther, Solomon, Curtis, Bob, Bruce, Scott, Dan, Fred, and Fitzie. I have teed it up with all of these people and many more. If I named them all, the list would fill this page.

Interestingly, they have enriched my experience. Most have made a round fun, though not usually in a way that has reduced my score. Some of them have thoroughly pissed me off. Conversely, I am sure I have been

The game is best enjoyed with friends.

irksome myself. Not unusual considering the millennia of practice we humans have in irritating our friends and neighbors.

Some of my golfing foursomes have included people who shall not be recognized here by their real names. I am assigning descriptive terms to identify them. Perhaps you have met up with them on your own golf course. They include Coin Jingler, Line Stomper, Sneak Peeker, Yakky, Chronic Complainer, and Club Thrower.

Coin Jingler always has a fistful of quarters in his pants pocket. He ignores the coinage on the tee box and fairway, but for some reason shoves his hand into his pants when he gets to the green and fidgets with the quarters while pacing the putting surface. As players prepare to putt, Coin Jngler dutifully stands still, but his pocketed hand springs into action as the putters start their stroke. Glares his way go unnoticed.

Line Stompers are everywhere. Never mind that golf etiquette says we should never walk on the line of players' pending putts. Line Stompers are either ignorant of the unwritten rule, are blissfully unaware of other players' ball positions, or flat out don't give a hoot. Those who truly don't know better can be informed and educated. The unaware types typically apologize when told of their transgression. The others? Well, they often shrug and exclaim that people playing before we got to the green walked there too. Or they dismiss the point as irrelevant. I say it's not irrelevant when a 250-pound player plants a size twelve seven inches from the cup fifteen seconds before I putt.

Sneak Peeker is the player who edges behind putters as they line up their stroke. Getting a view of the putt is common and accepted. Sometimes, however, the preview attempt goes a step too far and Sneak Peeker is not sneaky enough to avoid entering players' peripheral vision.

Yakky simply never shuts up. On the tee, in the cart, standing over their own shots, and especially while you are standing over yours, Yakky tells stories, comments on current events, critiques your swing, and even tells you you hit your putt too hard when you darn well know you hit your putt too hard.

Chronic Complainer has high standards and lets you know how each shot could have been better. Complainer tells you the shot was fat or thin or shanked or otherwise missed even when everybody could clearly see it was fat or thin or shanked. What's more, Chronic Complainer can make all the others feel inferior by complaining about shots the others would be thrilled to own.

Club Thrower needs no introduction. We've seen them in action. Truth is, I have sometimes been a Club Thrower myself. Perhaps you have too. This is not to trivialize Club Thrower's impact on our game. The degree to which Club Thrower launches the club varies. There are full helicopters, javelin throws, and meek tosses. One Club Thrower I know whirled his driver high enough to lodge in an oak tree forty feet off the ground. We may laugh off Club Thrower's display of disgust, but it certainly can put a damper on the fun.

You know those people and others. But of course there is good in every opportunity golfers have to share four hours of swinging, cheering, cursing, scolding, sweating, shivering, and riding emotions from the sublime to the ridiculous. The greater good, of course, is the gain we get from human contact.

We are instinctively inclined to socialize. I haven't researched this, but I would not be surprised to learn a sociologist or two has done a paper about why people made a game out of swatting balls with sticks.

Foursomes, threesomes, and twosomes finish their rounds better off than they were on the first tee. We walk off the final green after tipping caps, shaking hands, and sometimes sharing hugs—ancient and accepted signs of respect and acknowledgment.

Someday all of us will sign our final scorecard. When we add up the grand total, we will almost certainly be over par in terms of strokes. We will all be winners, however, in the satisfaction we experienced in pursuing all golfers' unquestioned common goal: to do better with each new encounter with the stationary sphere on the grass at our feet.

CHAPTER 6
Hallowed turf

The names of certain places on our planet are almost always spoken in awe. Grand Canyon. Victoria Falls. Pyramids. Machu Picchu. Mount Everest. The Parthenon.

They are wondrous places, spectacular to the eye, and often associated with mystical powers, supernatural ancestors, and omnipotent deities.

Golf also has certain places with names that roll reverently off the tongues of fans. They speak of such places in the same manner that faithful people speak about heaven.

Augusta. Pebble Beach. St. Andrews. Pinehurst. Carnoustie. Medinah. Bethpage Black. Firestone. Inverness. Oakmont.

Nobody ever shouts, AUGUSTA! On the greens, in the bars, or driving in cars, people who speak of Augusta utter the word with admiration that teeters toward reverence. Imagine the greenside marshal's "Quiet" sign, and you know you must whisper Augusta. Or Oakmont. Or St. Andrews.

As the Grand Canyon is more than a hole in the ground and the Pyramids are more than piles of big stones, Augusta, St. Andrews, and other legendary golf courses are more than grassy pastures. They are hallowed turf, made holy by the men and women who have competed on them and the people who know the skill and grit required to master them.

The wonders of the world and the wonders of golf share so much, but the wonders of golf are altogether different in one important distinction.

We simply look at the world's wonders, while the hallowed fairways and greens invite us to experience them just as they were experienced by Morris, Ouimet, Jones, Sarazen, Hogan, Lopez, Palmer, Nicklaus, Woods, Sörenstam, and their brothers and sisters.

It was one o'clock in the afternoon that sunny July day when I walked to the first tee of Pebble Beach. I was up early that day, sipped coffee, strolled the grounds beyond the Inn at Spanish Bay, and imagineered myself walking around the fabled holes laid out along the beaches of Monterey Bay. Anticipation built as we drove onto the property, hit balls on the range, and practiced putts, all the while our tee time drawing near.

Our group that day is my favorite foursome: wife Barb, daughter Betsy, and her husband, Irfan. Our daughter and son-in-law had arranged for the bucket-list golf trip to commemorate my retirement. They arranged for it all—the cross-country flight and the unmatched hospitality at the inn to the tee times at the iconic courses and fabulous meal at The Tap Room overlooking Pebble's famous eighteenth green.

We soaked in the moment, standing at the first tee in awe of the fairway beyond as the starter provided instructions to us first-time Pebble Beach golfers. Then the time came, time to get real and face the challenges—the very same challenges with which the world's best golfers dealt en route to glorious victories, shattering defeats, and everlasting (or as long as people golf) fame.

My first shot that afternoon was like many in my day: not bad, but not great. My nervous fade found rough near a tree, necessitating a punch-out to the fairway, where I could pitch to the pin. I nearly holed the par putt, but left satisfied with a tap-in bogey on my first Pebble Beach hole.

The author's wife, Barb, poses next to the Donald Ross statue at his iconic Pinehurst Number 2.

Number 2 plays as a par five for the public. I one-putted for a birdie and felt a rush of adrenalin as I walked to the third tee at even par. The rush continued as I hit the third green, an elevated platform. Momentum was on my side, but a disappointing three putt quickly snapped me back to reality.

Though I swear it was right down the middle, my fourth-hole tee shot eluded discovery. I think a seabird snatched it, but Barb wasn't buying my theory. Frustration, the kind that haunts nearly every golfer regardless of talent, became my overarching emotion. I tried to sweep frustration aside by admiring the namesake beach, the undulating layout, the gentle waves lapping the rocky outcroppings, and the expansive blue Pacific.

But frustration won again on the treacherous hole Number 7, where I took two shots to escape the green-protecting bunker and three more to get the ball in the hole. I'm not the only one to card a six on seven, but that makes no never mind to me.

Hole 8 claimed the second shots of all four of us. I cannot recall anything from Hole 9 or 10, no doubt due to the brain fog of Number 8. I did make a one-putt par on 14. I never found my tee shot on 17 and ended my round with a string of bunker-to-bunker-to-bunker shots that resulted in an 8 on 18.

Other than that, it was a great day.

The next day at Spyglass, our tee time in the chilly morning fog, featured barking seals, grazing deer, and lots of bad shots, plus a couple of admonishments from the ranger to pick up our pace of play.

But who can complain, right? In hindsight, we shouldn't have even tried to keep score. Barb has our scorecards somewhere (she had low gross both days), but I really don't need to see them to reflect on those thirty-six holes of unforgettable golf.

I've also been up close and personal at Pinehurst, Firestone, The Greenbriar, Oakmont, and Crooked Stick. I have visited them and joined the galleries at major tournaments but not had the pleasure to play them. They are all special places. To borrow the aphorism, if you know, you know. They are hallowed turf. They are places with sod trod by the greats of the game and where the ghosts of golf can be heard whispering their magical names. Listen and you will hear. Hallowed indeed.

Walking in the footsteps of legends

It's one thing to walk the grounds at Augusta National as a spectator but quite another to be on the course itself in an official capacity.

Tennessee native James Thomas parlayed early work as a high school golfer, then caddie gigs and golf course food and beverage associate into an opportunity to caddie at the famous home of the Masters golf championship. Working out of the Augusta caddie shack, JT looped for a number of famous members, including billionaires Bill Gates and Warren Buffett and football coaching great Lou Holtz.

JT can regale you with stories of who's generous with the "stew" (tips) and who's stingy as well as the idiosyncrasies of the rich and famous. But when it comes to Augusta, golfers want to know what it feels like to walk the fairways and pace the greens.

"You really are walking hallowed grounds, but after five or ten times around there it does become second nature. You don't throw your cigar or cigarette on the ground there, for sure. If you do, you're never coming back," said JT. "Those pine trees you see on TV, the needles are so thick that they literally knock the ball down. When you hit it into the trees, nine times out of ten it's staying in them." Augusta aficionados know of Rae's Creek, the meandering waterway that influences scores on several critical holes.

"Every green breaks to Rae's Creek except 17, which is the most unreadable green out there," he said.

What is misunderstood about Augusta? "The membership," said JT. "You can have all the money in the world, but if you're not invited, you're not a member."

The author's wife, Barb, and daughter, Betsy, get ready to tee it up at Pebble Beach's Hole 7, with Monterey Bay as the backdrop.

CHAPTER 7

The greatest golf coach of all time

Spoiler alert: This is just my opinion. I have no numbers to justify my ranking, no won-loss record to convince you of my choice. It's just my opinion.

So I don't feel as though I'm going out on a limb here when I tell you who I believe is the greatest golf coach of all time. But first, I will tell you it is not Butch Harmon or David Leadbetter. It's not Jim McLean or Dave Pelz. Nor is it Harvey Penick.

They all are good, even great. So is Ted Ossoff, the owner of a hardscrabble nine-hole track in Columbiana, Ohio, who counted me among his students, along with LPGA Hall of Famer Dottie Pepper.

But I'm telling you here and now that I know the greatest golf coach—and I know her well. She's flattered but mortified that I'm making this pronouncement, but what the hell, it's my opinion, and that's all that matters.

She is Barb Woods Wollitz. I am married to Coach Wollitz—or Barb, as her players called her. In my opinion, biased though it might be, Barb has done as much for her players as just about anyone has for theirs. Her contributions are not measured in championships or winning seasons. Her players did not advance to professional status. In fact, most of them moved on to college studies and nongolf careers, marriages, motherhood, and other joys that enrich the lives of young women.

Barb coached girls' golf teams at two high schools over a twenty-year span. Herself a high school golfer in the days when the sport was starting

24

Retired high school girls' golf coach Barb Wollitz with graduated Salem
Quaker golfers Lindsay Winn Gates and Kristen Rhodes Tooley.

to gain traction among teenage girls, Barb stepped up in 1997 when our
daughter, Betsy, told her no team existed for girl golfers in our suburban
high school. Betsy aspired to tee it up for her school.

"Really?" Barb said. "We'll see about that."

So Barb went to work, coaxed the athletic director to authorize a club
team, and gathered a band of teen girls with the combined experience
of just a bit more than zero years. A year later, the AD upped the team
to official scholastic league competition, and the Lady Bulldogs went to
work.

Two years later, Betsy graduated and moved on to Miami University,
and Barb joined forces with friend Jill Harmon to start the girls' golf
team at Salem (Ohio) High School. Their Quakers had a couple of
experienced players, but for the most part, the team was composed of

young girls juggling marching band practice, schoolwork, babysitting, and chores at home.

After Jill stepped down to focus on her business, Barb became the sole coach and earned coach of the year recognition in her interscholastic conference. Her teams featured players with spirit and determination but often short on natural talent.

None of this really mattered much to Barb. They were her "golf children," and she loved them dearly. For twenty years, she met wide-eyed eighth graders who dreamed they might play on a varsity squad, welcomed them as freshmen a year later, coached and guided them for four years, and sent them off as eighteen-year-old women who had accomplished something most of them never dreamed they could do.

To say Barb's teams were short on experience is an understatement. She came home after the first day of tryouts every summer with the same story: "I asked a new freshman how long she'd been playing. She said she started last week!"

During her tenure as the Salem coach, Barb also drove the team van. Competing in a conference spread across two counties, the Quakers often had rides to away matches that lasted an hour on twisting country roads. That's an eternity in a cramped van filled with teens eager to learn about life and share their experiences.

Though the conversations sometimes made her cringe, Barb heeded the pledge "What's said in the van stays in the van."

And so it did.

But the result of Barb's twenty years of coaching girls growing into young women was the opportunity to lend a bit of her unique perspective to the experience of her players. I saw it from the edge of the fairways, the tears of failure, the high fives of success, and the heartfelt hugs. I saw it at several of her players' weddings and saw it in the grin on the face of a former player who introduced her own child to her former coach.

As I observed Barb's style and manner with her golf children, I saw she was doing something way more important than trying to guide kids to shoot winning scores. She was an advocate and ally for her players navigating bumpy teen years. She instilled an appreciation for respect of the game, integrity in competition, and support for each other.

Their scores were one thing. But the real thing was the quality of the women—the Bulldogs and Quakers—who took golf-learned lessons with them to their lives after high school.

Like I said, it's just my opinion, and the scorecards don't show it, but she is the greatest golf coach of all time.

Author Jack Wollitz and Coach Barb Wollitz with Salem Quaker golfer Kelly Hutton on her way to playing for the Youngstown State University women's team

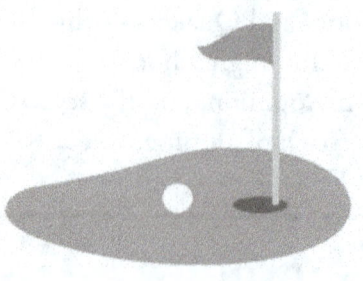

CHAPTER 8

Collared shirts required

In the overall scheme of things, what one decides to wear on a golf course would seem to be relatively unimportant compared with whether we follow the rules or possess enough eye-hand coordination to properly strike the golf ball.

But indeed it matters a great deal. While cheaters and hackers tee it up daily all around the world, guys who show up at the first tee wearing cargo shorts, collarless shirts or tank tops may very well be sent home or to the pro shop to buy suitable attire. Ladies' shirts showing midriff skin or revealing too much cleavage and shorts too short also are no-nos (though I for one believe they add to the beauty of the game). I don't necessarily object, but I do find it curious that pants with big pockets sewn on their outsides are considered counter to polite golf attire.

Well then, I consider that times change. It is possible some day men may tee up with armpit hair on full display and women may shed their modesty to maximize their tummy tans. It was not too long ago, after all, that ladies played golf in long skirts and high-top shoes and their menfolk sported neckties and tweed coats.

Golf fashion is a huge industry. I am no expert. I can only tell you what I see, what I like, and what I think.

Most sports have uniforms, which I find to be important for fans. Sure, the players need to recognize their teammates, so wearing shirts of the same color makes sense. Baseball teammates wear matching hats. Football players wear matching helmets. You get the picture.

Uniforms also are important for the fans. Certainly it helps focus your energy when you're cheering "Go! Fight! Win!" to people wearing the same colors. I recall comedian Jerry Seinfeld's quip about fans who, when it's all said and done, are really cheering for their favorite clothing.

I have little knowledge of ancient athletes, but I suspect they wore what was available, stuff easy to buy off-the-rack and readily disposable, since there were no clubhouse staffers to launder out the blood and spit of vanquished foes.

As ancient times ebbed past the midpoint of the past millennium, people found fun in swatting balls around meadows, pastures, and beaches and counting the number of whacks they took before the ball rolled into a hole. We're told the early golf game evolved in places where the air was cold, the wind blew hard, and rain fell frequently. So early golfers' clothing was exactly what they would wear when they went to meadows, pastures, and beaches on chilly, windy, rainy days. Go figure.

Save for events such as the Ryder and Solheim and other cup events, golf is mostly contested between individuals rather than teams. So like-looking clothing is unnecessary to distinguish one side from another. Nevertheless, a look has evolved.

The look, in fact, is noteworthy not just because of the style du jour. A golfer friend of my daughter at Worthington Hills Country Club near Columbus, Ohio, recently observed, "Golf is the only sport where the fans dress exactly like the players, just in case we need to jump in."

Indeed.

For men, the look starts with a shirt that has a collar and sleeves. For women, sleeves and collars are curiously optional. Hats run the gamut, with the decided favorite among men being baseball-style caps. Some courses, including my club in Naples, stipulate that ball caps must be worn with the bill facing forward.

Lady players often went hatless before visors became popular, but LPGA golfer Michelle McGann made stylish hats with wide brims and ribbons popular in the 1990s.

Since the dawn of professional play, male golfers were required to compete in long pants. Then LIV golf took wing, and short pants became a statement of differentiation versus PGA tournaments.

In this era of hyper athleticism displayed in everything from sculpted physiques to performance clothing, golf shoes look far more like athletic footwear than the hard-soled, stiff leather oxford and saddle shoes from the days of yore. Remember those fringed flapping kilties on golf shoes? Popular styles today are kiltie free, save for those seeking a retro look.

Look back twenty years and you'll see golf clothing you wouldn't be caught wearing on a course today. It's a good guess twenty years from now golfers will be wearing fashions much removed from the standard stuff of 2026.

God forbid, however, that we will bear witness to hirsute shoulders revealed by tank-topped golfers in 2046. Some things are best left unseen.

This shirt may be covered with birds, but its collar makes it pass golf courses' dress codes.

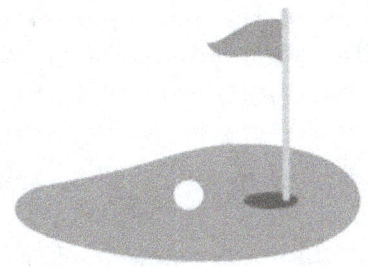

CHAPTER 9

Aces in the hole

Many years ago, I worked for a man who scored a hole in one. He was a frequent golfer, playing out of a bag that looked as though it belonged to Jackie Gleason in his Honeymooners TV days. Steve was his name, and he played around nine or ten a.m. with his wife on weekdays when they could sneak away from their mom-and-pop gas station. I worked there summers and after school.

I was on the job the day Steve returned to his shop beaming a smile from lips clenching the stump of his smoldering R. G. Dunn cigar. Steve often popped into the garage expecting he would need to restore order from chaos created by employees left unsupervised for several hours. That day, however, Steve seemed to be unconcerned about unfinished repair work, greasy floors, and rag-littered workbenches.

"See this?" he said as he held out a golf ball. "I got a hole in one this morning!" His pride was on full display. The scene begged for a ball-busting comment from one of his employees.

"You lucky SOB!"

"Luck, hell!" Steve exclaimed. "I was aiming for the hole."

The most celebrated shot in golf is the hole in one, also known as an ace. Most aces are par three tee shots that are holed out. Par three aces are not the rarest shots. That distinction goes to the double eagle, or albatross, which is the hole out of the second shot on a par five.

But aces are and have been universally celebrated, and for good reason. They make good rounds better. They often turn bad rounds into unforgettable rounds. They prove, if for only one shot, that the golfer is worthy. They are rare enough to stand out. And they are reasons to pour drinks and soak in congratulations.

Some say aces are luck. Perhaps. But as Steve pointed out many years ago, those who record a hole in one are shooting for the flag, after all.

Mr. Google says the odds of a common golfer holing a tee shot are 1 in 12,500. The PGA of America reports between 1 and 2 percent of golfers card aces annually, and one quarter of them are between the ages of fifty and fifty-nine. That suggests experience is a factor.

The average handicap of those scoring holes in one is fourteen. That suggests luck is a factor.

I know excellent golfers who have never aced. I know high handicappers who have several. One of my friends aced a ninety-yard par three with her driver, lighting off a celebration every bit as festive as for the friend whose ace came on a 190-yard hole.

That's the cool thing about holes in one. Anybody can get one. They are always fun. And they are best enjoyed in the company of friends.

Word reached me recently that my friend Nancy Card knocked in her seventh career ace. It happened on the fourth hole of our club, Glen Eagle, in Naples, Florida, the third time she's aced that hole. She teed it up in thick fog, aimed where she thought the pin might be, pulled

Dave Tenaglia knocked in his tee shot at Hole 4 on Glen Eagle in Naples, Florida.

the trigger, and bingo! She didn't actually see her ball roll into the hole, but it doesn't matter because she got to mark 1 in the box. She also has experienced the supremely rare thrill of two aces in one round.

I have witnessed several noteworthy aces, two by my wife, Barb. I was with her for her first at Deer Creek in Ohio and her second at Foxfire in Pinehurst, North Carolina. I was elsewhere when her tee shot rolled into the hole on Number 6 at Glen Eagle. Over the years I've watched from the tee when Jimmy DeCapita and Rich Getch aced at Mohawk Trails in Pennsylvania, Cosmo Pecchia knocked one in at Knoll Run in Ohio, and Dave Tenaglia dropped one at Glen Eagle.

The rub of certain greens would up the odds for aces. One hole, in particular, was notorious for rewarding accurate pin shots: The old Number 16 at Hubbard Golf Course in Ohio's Trumbull County. Locals knew it as the Saucer Hole thanks to its bowl-shaped green that drained balls toward the center. The pin was often smack dab in the middle. The green itself was elevated and protected by bunkers, so golfers on the sixteenth tee box could not see the putting surface. But any shot that found the green—left, right, short or long—could reasonably be expected to trickle close to the hole. Pars were easy, birdies were common, and aces were frequent enough to earn the 120-yard Saucer Hole the reputation of offering golfers their best chance to score a 1.

It is said the Saucer Hole delivered more than one thousand holes in one before the golf course changed hands and became known as Pine Lakes and the new owner decided to renovate the old parkland-style course. One of the changes he made along with golf course designer Brian Huntley was a new Number 16. It is a beautiful conventional par three with a lake, bunkers, and pin placements easily viewed by golfers lining up their tee shots. It has had its share of aces since debuting in 2008, but the odds are definitely higher than for those who played the old Saucer Hole.

Luck and more were on my side when I scored five holes in one. Three of them, in fact, were poor shots that against all odds found the bottom of the cup. Two, I am proud to say, were the outcome of great shots, maybe even brilliant, if I may be permitted to say (here I want you to imagine the laughing-face emoji as punctuation).

My most recent ace is super fresh in my mind. It happened just yesterday—March 16, 2025—during a round at Glen Eagle with friends preceding a corned beef-and-cabbage St. Patrick's Day dinner party. The wind was gusting, bursts topping 25 miles per hour. The distance was 100 yards. I pulled out my pitching wedge, lined up the shot, waggled, and lofted the ball to ride the left-to-right wind. It dropped three feet from the hole, rolled, and dropped out of sight. Our celebration was without restraint and reached the disbelieving ears of Barb and her three friends playing immediately in front of us. As luck would have it, Barb aced the same hole eleven months prior.

Tradition calls for those who card aces to buy a round in the clubhouse. For some, it may be a quiet celebration limited to your foursome, perhaps forty dollars covering it all. For others, it may be in a raucous grille room where people you've never met suddenly appear to offer a toast to your success (at your expense). The cost can escalate quickly, which is the reason one friend is steadfast in his hope to never score another ace.

Bar tabs aside, to all my friends who have experienced the thrill of a hole in one, I say congratulations! To those who are still trying for number one, I say keep swinging. You never know when the hole will get in the way of a rolling golf ball.

The author, second from left, celebrates his ace at Glen Eagle's Hole 6 with St. Patrick's Day teammates Leo Rajter, Paul Krajewski, and Bob Marcoux.

CHAPTER 10

At home with
Donald Ross

South of Youngstown, Ohio, on the edge of a primordial forest 3,500 miles from the heaths and heather of the game's birthplace, sprawl thirty-six holes of golf magnificence.

The track is the muni beloved by local residents and a growing number of visiting golfers who come to play two of famed golf course designer and builder Donald Ross's finest layouts.

The Mill Creek Metroparks's thirty-six holes of classic Ross golf are the North Course and younger sister South Course. Pride runs deep among Youngstowners for the gems created for them by the legendary Ross, starting with Director of Golf Brian Tolnar and Golf Professional Stacie Butler.

Ross designed around four hundred courses, the most celebrated of which is US Open venue Pinehurst No. 2. There he became head golf professional in 1900 and won three North and South Opens. So what is so special about his two Mill Creek Metroparks layouts?

"Number one, it is special because the majority of the courses he designed are mostly private clubs," Tolnar said. "It was unusual for him to come and do a public course like Mill Creek."

Work on the front nine of the North Course began in 1926. After the North was opened in the summer of 1928, he returned to design and build the third nine (now the front side of the South Course). By 1931, the South was opened for play.

Mill Creek will celebrate its centennial in 2028.

"Thirty-six holes makes us unique among Donald Ross courses," Butler said. She and Tolnar said it's noteworthy that Ross chose to come to Youngstown, but it made sense considering his travel preferences.

"We are fortunate we were near a major railroad," Tolnar said. "Donald Ross didn't fly, so his courses usually were near railroads. It was not uncommon for him to work on two or three courses at a time. He was working on a course in Pittsburgh and going to Inverness in Toledo when he heard about the opportunity to build Mill Creek, which was directly on the route between the two cities."

After inspecting the terrain designated for the Mill Creek park system's new golf courses, Ross worked his magic with the rolling ground and tall trees on the North Course acreage.

The South Course is relatively flat, spread out across the land from which the namesake Mill Creek springs and flows. "South," as it is known colloquially, has been selected by *Golfweek* as one of America's thirty best municipal courses.

His thirty-six holes include a variety of natural hazards and more than one hundred cursed sand traps.

Mill Creek literature quotes Ross as saying, "There is no such thing as a misplaced bunker. Regardless of where a bunker may be, it is the business of the player to avoid it."

Tolnar said Ross was well-known for following the natural terrain. "We're not very hilly. We sit on the lowest point in Mahoning County."

The lowland setting could have been problematic, but Ross had a clever solution for the potentially boggy grounds.

"Donald Ross was ahead of his time as he built greens that would easily dry out," Tolnar said. "And his bunkers don't have high lips."

Butler noted the subtle optics that influence golfers' views and perspectives.

"When you are on his greens and look back down the fairway, you don't see the bunkers," she said. "And when you are on the course looking forward, you see everything in front of you, including the greens as they slope from back to front."

Mill Creek North and South also have their special Ross features known as chocolate drops. They are moguls that sweeten the golfers' view between the sixth and sixteenth holes on the South Course and twelfth and thirteenth holes on North. Chocolate drops became Ross trademarks as he continued developing courses throughout the US.

Known today for its parkland setting and tall hardwood trees, Mill Creek presented a challenge for those tasked with clearing space for fairways and greens. Heavy equipment was not as easy to come by in the 1920s, so teams of horses had to be harnessed to drag trees and pull stumps.

It's interesting to note that if you were standing on the tee of the first hole on North, you would see no trees on the right. Trees there now grew from saplings in the 1920s.

Donald Ross left his mark at Mill Creek, and Mill Creek is making sure nobody forgets it. Tolnar and Butler market Mill Creek's Ross connection vigorously. Ross's picture is in all thirty-six hole cups and every cart and is printed on the scorecards and displayed at the indoor player development center.

Mill Creek in Youngstown, Ohio, proudly displays its Donald Ross heritage everywhere, including inside all thirty-six cups.

"We really try to make sure everybody who comes on the property knows we're a Donald Ross course," Butler said.

Tolnar added, "Donald Ross is brought up more than you might think. We are members of the Donald Ross Society, and they support our grant requests for our various improvement projects.

"People are really interested. We get groups who travel the country to play Donald Ross courses."

I have played Mill Creek North and South for decades. Recent upgrades have resulted in improved grass and bunker conditions, restored tee boxes, more natural areas, and generally better aesthetics as the course ages toward its one hundredth year.

Throughout it all, Mill Creek's eighteen-hole layouts are two of the busiest courses in a region blessed with affordable premium golf.

"Before I came here, I worked twelve years in Rochester, New York. If you picked up and moved Mill Creek to Rochester, you'd pay $150 on weekends. Here we charge $34 for seniors to play eighteen holes in a cart," Tolnar said.

Butler said both eighteens are equally popular.

"We have a lot of leagues that play here, and they can have a different nine every week April through October. Each nine is different, with more trees on the South and more demanding greens on the North," she said.

In addition to hosting public and league play, Mill Creek is the home course for eight high school teams and the Youngstown State University men's and women's intercollegiate teams.

To keep pace with the demand and passage of time, Mill Creek is in the midst of a ten-year plan for more than $8 million in upgrades.

"We are on pace to be wrapped up in spring 2028 in time for the centennial. We will be completing the modernization of our irrigation project, patching and replacing where necessary to eliminate any brown spots and installing more sprinklers so tees and greens have multiple heads. The work is a game changer for the property and will preserve it for the next one hundred years," Tolnar said.

Butler said, "We really are fortunate here in Youngstown. A lot of people play here every year and don't realize how lucky we are to have such a gem here. We are fortunate to have thirty-six holes of Donald Ross so affordable and still top quality."

The efforts of Butler, Tolnar, Superintendent Lance Bailey, the grounds crews, and the MetroParks board and administration are gaining attention well beyond Youngstown and Mahoning County.

Tolnar estimates marketing at golf and travel shows in Toronto, New York, Michigan, New Jersey, and Pennsylvania as well as nearby Cleveland, promoting stay-and-play packages, has brought in thousands of additional rounds.

Everybody wants to experience the same Ross course that brought Hall of Fame golfer Sam Snead to Youngstown.

Who was Donald Ross?

Born in Dornoch, Scotland, Donald Ross learned golf and golf course design from Old Tom Morris at St. Andrews. In addition to his fame as a golf course architect, he was an accomplished golfer who carded top ten finishes in the US Open and the Open Championship. Ross came to the US. just before the turn to the twentieth century and maintained his professional playing status throughout his design career.

Ross was known for turtleback and double plateau greens. He built courses without moving a lot of dirt and favored greens where a golfer could run a shot onto the green but also risk running over the back.

He was said to believe in designing a new course with the thought to make each hole present a different problem. He sought to build each hole so that it wasted none of the ground and enabled him "to capitalize on every possibility I saw."

In a word, Ross was "imaginative."

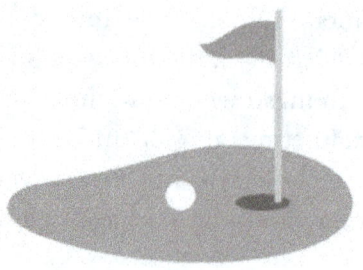

CHAPTER 11

A track for every hacker

In my judgment, there is something grand about every golf course.

That may be a big claim, but I believe it to be true. I am not limiting the field to the classics, the famous, the oldest, or the toughest. Regardless of the superlatives a golfer might apply in describing golf courses, each is distinctive. That makes them special, if not in the eyes of the masses at least in the opinions of those who love them.

Consider that every course has a creator. It could be Donald Ross, Robert Trent Jones, Pete Dye, or Old Tom Morris. Or it could be a farmer who grew weary of rotating his three hundred acres between corn and soybeans so he traded his tractor for a bulldozer and pushed dirt into piles to be graded into greens.

Interestingly, the finest golf courses have critics, and the worst courses have fans. There are always some who will nitpick, and there are always those who will be delighted.

Regardless of the quality of the grass, the precision of the mowers, the craftiness of the designer, and the degree of difficulty, the objective is always to get around the track with as few strokes as possible. The game is the same at Scotland's Carnoustie as it is at the VFW club on the outskirts of town.

Donald Ross may have had a special eye for undulations and for protecting greens. Pete Dye certainly loved his railroad ties. Jack Nicklaus is known for wide fairways and maintaining much of the land's natural features. Some designers incorporate deep bunkers and thick rough in their layouts, but some have zero sand traps and crew-cut rough. Farmer

Brown's hand-sketched course design might have all or any of the features made famous by the game's greatest minds.

There is no rule about the total yardage or even the number of par threes, fours, and fives. If they add up to nine or eighteen holes, that's typically good enough, but some developers are laying out twelve-hole tracks for those who must hurry through their rounds.

Around my hometown, Youngstown, Ohio, dozens of golf courses open at sunrise every day and play host to thousands of people. Golf options in Youngstown range from top-shelf to hardscrabble. I have tried almost all of the courses within fifty miles of home and can honestly say each is unique in its own special way.

This is not to say I love all of them. Yes, I do have my favorites. But all of them, I suppose, are favorite places for somebody out there because they are patronized by people who walk up to the counter with cash or credit card in hand to pay the greens fee and partake in whatever challenge the courses have to offer.

It may not be apparent at first glance, but each is special in ways that only their players can know. It could be the steep incline of the first fairway, the wooded backdrop at Number 6, or the oak tree guarding the front of the seventh green. Perhaps it's the pond to the right of twelve's fairway or maybe the teeny tiny seventeenth green. "Special" is indeed in the eyes of the golfer, whether it's banter with

Easy or tough, picturesque or scratchy, every golf course has a loyal corps of players.

the staff, the tree-lined fairways, or even the hotdogs in the clubhouse.

For me and for many, the grandeur of golf courses often is reserved for the eighteenth hole. From the fairways of many, golfers approaching the greens are rewarded with a spectacular view of the green complex with stately clubhouses posed as the backdrop.

I never gave this much thought until twenty years ago when I noticed the big white house perched on the hill behind the ninth and eighteenth greens at River Falls Plantation in Duncan, South Carolina. Such a sight for weary eyes with its 100-foot-wide porch so perfect for sipping iced tea after a muggy round or celebrating success (or survival) with a cold beer and good friends.

Walk with me and see the sprawling clubhouse just beyond the eighteenth at Pinehurst. Would Nicklaus's Muirfield be Muirfield without the house on the crest behind eighteen to pull weary golfers up the last of so many steep inclines? Oakmont's clubhouse beckons likewise, as do the grand buildings behind the home holes of Oxmoor Ridge in Birmingham, Alabama, The Quarry in Canton, Ohio, and so many others for golfers ready for the rewards of even finishing their rounds.

Architecture, layout, condition, location, terrain, and more all factor into the grandeur of every golf course I can recall. St. Andrews Old Course has its Road Hole, Firestone its Monster, and Augusta its, well, everywhere one looks Augusta is grand, grander, or grandest.

For my weekday grasshoppers group, grand views, challenges, and rewards await every Monday, Wednesday, and Friday. We love the parkland setting of Mill Creek's North and South courses, the splendidly challenging water shot to Reserve Run's eighth hole, the confoundingly difficult ninth and eighteenth at Yankee Run, and the rarely parred first at Kennsington.

Across America and around the world, we truly do have a track for every hacker, each special in ways millions may agree but only you can say for sure.

CHAPTER 12
The Perch on Number 7

As I write this, four women are approaching their second shots on the seventh fairway. It sprawls left and right across my field of view from my perch on the third floor of our seasonal home in Naples, Florida.

They are Janet, Patty, Jane, and Joyce. Waiting back on the tee box are Maureen, Nancy, Mary Lynn, and Barb. I know them all; some turn and wave as they play through, guessing correctly that I am watching from my most excellent vantage point.

A light rain is falling, but the fairway ladies all strike nice shots, as do the foursome off the tee behind them. They accomplished what untold thousands of golfers before them also accomplished at the same club: they succeeded in advancing on their missions to hole out on the seventh green of Glen Eagle Golf & Country Club.

So it goes from seven thirty every morning to dusk every evening. A parade of golfers swings through their rounds at our October-through-April home and club in Naples. They begin, they proceed, and they conclude.

But they do not all do it the same. That's golf. You play your way. I'll play mine. Some take four shots to finish number seven at Glen Eagle. I believe more than some take five, six, seven, even eight. A few take three.

Scores, however, are not the only thing happening on the slight-dogleg-left seventh hole. It is Trouble with a capital T. A lake looms off the tee. Out-of-bounds stretches the entirety of the right side. A dense palmetto and pine penalty area threatens to swallow balls yanked or pushed left off the tee. A fairway bunker eats nearly half of each day's tee shots.

I know this because I see it with my own eyes from my perch thirty feet above the midpoint of Number 7. Plus, I've played it umpteen times, mostly with an overpar outcome.

I have watched all manner of shenanigans from my lofty viewpoint. Course rules require that balls resting on the crushed coquina shells cart path are to be played as they lie. Most players nevertheless take relief but not the requisite stroke. Many shots come to rest in the out-of-bounds Bermuda grass so thick that finding balls is difficult. We can see them from our perch and, when we're in the mood, guide players to their lost balls. Though the balls are clearly OB, some players address the ball, wiggle, waggle, and swing through the thick blades in attempts to return to the fairway without counting the penalty stroke. Most toss their OB balls back into play, but I'm sure more than a few "forget" to count stroke

Periodic palm pruning clears the view for those who watch from The Perch.

and distance.

Balls that come to rest with a white OB stake impeding a full swing have all kinds of resolutions—most of them not within the rules. Apparently unfamiliar with the white-stake rule, many players remove the offending stick and swing for the green. More than a few call over to their buddies that their ball is fine as they foot wedge it from the OB stake. A fairly significant number of players, upon discovering their ball in the out-of-bounds Bermuda, look to see whether anybody is looking and toss balls back in play with notice to their foursome, "All good over here."

Then there is that bunker. It's a score-destroying predicament—for some, but not for all. We have a clear view of bunkered shots from The Perch. We also have a clear line of sight to players who kick balls out of the sand, ground their clubs, or lift balls from fried-egg lies, and anything else that might come to mind as they deal with the hazard without pain or suffering.

The eight women I introduced at the top of this chapter did none of the atrocities cited above. I watched them play appropriately, with a brisk and measured pace, and with compliments to their friends whose shots deserved praise. Admirable.

This is not to say we who watch from The Perch are not always silent sentinels.

What's sport without a little heckling? Friends who play through our view typically get a shout-out greeting. Those we know as good sports might generate a wisecrack or false praise. "Is that all you got?" And, in homage to Arnold Palmer's iconic line in the USGA TV commercial against slow play, "While we're young!"

From The Perch we see all and, with haughty judgment, compliment or condemn.

So remember as you continue your life of golf, somebody is watching you from a perch with an excellent vantage point. You may not feel their gaze, but they see what you're doing. Give them something to admire.

CHAPTER 13

Whose swing is that?

The first time I ever saw my swing on video was an awakening. For decades, I had imagined my swing as a long, languid motion with a full takeaway and turn, balanced transition descending to extended arms delivering power provided by hips, thighs, and knees. My footwork was perfect, and the follow-through was complete down to my belt buckle pointing down the fairway to the flag.

I played for years with this vision of my golf swing bouncing between my ears. Then I bought a camcorder. I took it to a driving range, and Barb set up behind me to record my practice session.

The video certainly was an awakening. A rude awakening, in fact. I was horrified by the evidence on the tape. Who was that guy? Where was the perfectly balanced, shoulder-turning, weight-shifting swinger? The guy I saw was a falling-off-his-back-leg, lucky-to-make-contact hacker. My vision had been a delusion.

That's when I realized I really am a common golfer. Few swings are perfect. Mine falls into the far-from-perfect category. In fact, it never was what I had imagined. I'm not forty anymore, and I passed fifty and sixty a while back, and seventy just recently, so the bad habits I had in days gone by are exacerbated today by the passage of time and its deleterious effects on bones, muscles, tendons, ligaments, and the most important body part of the golfer, the brain.

Golf, says my friend Jim Plessinger, is a lot like bowling. He should know. He competed on the Pro Bowlers Tour for a few years and owned and operated a popular bowling center in York, Pennsylvania. We chatted about the golf swing during a recent round at our club in Naples, Florida.

"In golf and in bowling, it's all about leverage and timing," Jim explained while driving to our second shots, both (miraculously for me) in the fairway. "Leverage and timing. Whether we're swinging a golf club or rolling a bowling ball, it's about getting our shoulders and hands, hips and feet in perfect timing so we can generate the leverage necessary to put the ball where we want it to go."

Leverage and timing? Easier said than done. I'm not a great golfer, but I'm also a terrible bowler. So if and when I sync my leverage and timing, it's probably accidental.

Recently golf buddies have advised, "Jack, you need to make a full turn and rotate your shoulder and hips through the shot."

Yeah, I know that.

Many have tried, and all have failed, to get my creaky frame to execute the takeaway, transition, hip drive, and follow-through that delivers long and accurate golf shots. Golf pros like Ted Ossoff, Andy Costa, Mike Shulas, Lucas Muzzey, Paige Cavalier, and the late Don Vandermillen have watched, analyzed, and instructed. Ossoff, who helped Dottie Pepper swing her way into the LPGA Hall of Fame, impressed his centrifugal force teachings on me with the swinging-bucket-on-a-rope analogy. He tried his best. But here I am today, my buddies' jabs echoing in my ears.

As a matter of fact, my lousy golf swing did not happen by accident. I trace it back to my storied career in youth baseball. I was the kid with a decent arm and willingness to crouch bravely before a batted baseball bouncing over a ragtag dirt-and-stones infield. I could take one off the chest, glove it, and throw to first base in time to nip the runner.

My bat was another story. I played organized ball from ages nine to sixteen, but I do not ever recall a round-the-bases home run. My swing produced contact, and the hits I recorded were ground balls through holes (and under fielders' gloves), along with line drives to right center. I stroked my share of singles and doubles with a short swing that really never finished with the hips-generated roundhouse, wraparound follow-through of my baseball hero Rocky Colavito. I spent hours every summer imagining myself as the Rock, swinging at phantom pitches in the driveway and imagining towering home runs clearing the fence at cavernous Cleveland

Every swing is different. Some, like this one, work well.

Municipal Stadium. That, unfortunately, was not the swing I took to the dusty diamonds of sandlot ball.

Nor, it turns out, was it the swing I took to the golf course I played with neighborhood friend Tom Oliphant and his father. Here's the thing: I didn't know any better. I believed I was as fluid as the pros I watched on the television broadcasts of *Shell's Wonderful World of Golf*. I believed when I went on a golf tournament date with future wife Barb that my swing might mirror the ones I witnessed from the gallery at Firestone Country Club in Akron as Ray Floyd notched a World Series of Golf victory.

Mercifully, my ignorance was bliss. I knew not the hitches and glitches, so I was spared the reality that my clunky swings were the reasons par was such an elusive score.

Then came the day when Barb shouldered the family camcorder, pushed the record button, and taped the swing I had no idea was mine. My delusion of grandeur was dashed. It was so painfully obvious why 280 yards was out of reach and why my tee shots were topped, sliced, and popped up. As the tape rolled on, the swings I saw seemed to be by someone other than me.

Still I play. Golfers must golf because we know the day will come when the swing becomes nearly what we envision. The truth is sometimes we do figure it out, and the video will prove what we've always suspected. And that is that we really do know how to strike the ball like a winner.

CHAPTER 14

Practice makes (almost) perfect

By now, you know this book is not an instructional manual. Nor is it based on the theories, tips, and training by professional golfers and legendary teachers. Rather, these pages are all about the common golfer.

Meet Jim Zarlenga.

His friends call him Zar. He is a retired math teacher, counselor, coach, and referee. He also is a golfer, and a pretty good one for sure, though not the best player I know. He can shoot his age—something most of us will never do—and take our money.

I know better golfers, but when I thought about this chapter, the first name that popped into my head was Jim Zarlenga. That is because he practices more purposely and precisely than any seventy-something amateur grandpa golfer I know. He is the epitome of the common golfer who strives for uncommon success.

Interestingly, he talks about the game like I would imagine he lectured his math students. He is eager to share and happy to teach. We started our conversation with one simple request: let's talk about good practice.

It is a fact that Zar arrives at the golf course not only prepared to win, but convinced victory is his. Before he pulls into the parking lot, he's ready because he has invested time in visualizing like an engineer, choreographing like a dancer, working muscles like a boxer, and focusing on positivity like an optimist.

His first words covered the mental aspect. You probably have heard similar advice. Common though it may be, the advice is worth repeating.

"Golf is played between your ears," said Zar. "Before you swing the club out there, you have to have thoughts about what you're going to do that day. You don't have to shoot for the sixties. What you're thinking has to be realistic. To play well, you first have to believe you will play well."

The value of positive thinking cannot be overstated.

"If you think negatively, you'll probably produce a negative shot. Golf has lots of do's and don'ts. I prefer the do's. I don't want to be around negative people. I remind my friends, like when they are standing by water and they reach for an old ball, that they are thinking negative thoughts about putting their ball in the water."

He believes big time in visualizing the upcoming shots, offering his own vivid advice.

"Playing any shot in my mind has to have color. I visualize my white ball bouncing on the green putting surface with a red flag. The details help you create a positive visual.

"For instance, the third hole at Knoll Run [a course we both play often]. I think of a white golf ball flying at a certain height, even higher so it will stay where it lands. Then I watch it hit the green next to the red flag. The more detailed you think, the better you will score."

He is an advocate of watching, studying, and mimicking the good swings he sees on televised professional tournaments.

"Pick a golfer closely aligned with your body type. For example, my body is similar to Jordan Spieth's, though I'm a little shorter, so I watch his swing a lot and practice what he does. You need to have somebody with you when you practice. You can't see your swing. You have to feel your swing. You need to see if you're casting or your elbows are too loose. If I cut that ball, it's because my elbow was flying."

Zar even shared a bit of advice for Spieth. "One thing, he's hard on himself. His coach should talk to him about being nicer to himself."

Watching pro golfers also provides hints about preparation.

"When you see pro golfers stand behind the ball for a few seconds, they are visualizing what they are going to do. Each shot is different, so they stand back to visualize what they will actually be doing. Then, when they're prepared, they do it."

Zar passed along his love of golf to son Josh, a collegiate player who works hard on his game.

"My son has a simulator, but I don't go there often. It's his place. Instead, I practice in my own basement. This morning, I grabbed one of the two putters I use a lot and did my normal routine. I drop a ball and create a target spot, like two parentheses, then putt through the channel in the spot to the 'hole.' If I miss the spot, it is because I moved my eyes or head. I focus on a place on the ball—a word, color, letter—not thinking about alignment, the shot, or other stuff, but instead thinking about the hole itself. If I'm too focused on the shot itself, the execution is great, but I will end up dead short. My practice strokes must be rehearsals of how hard to hit it. I have to think of that cup."

To the steel beams in his basement, Zar attaches heavy rubber bands with grips.

"I start by pulling through like I'm hitting a shot, using a slow, steady swing like the follow-through. Then I go in reverse to do the takeaway. It's hard to pull because those rubber bands are really taut. I go low

Jim Zarlenga takes his own advice and adheres to a practical practice regimen.

and slow, exercising the muscles, flexing the hips. I work the swing even though I'm not playing the game. I turn, right hip back, then flip to the left hip, and then face my target, hands finishing high. I do that a lot without a club in my hand, just to rehearse what I'm going to do on the course, and watch the imaginary ball come off the club face."

Practice need not be a lonely existence. "Have someone help you, to tell you what you're doing wrong, someone who knows you and your game."

Like all common golfers, Zar has had his share of experience in bunkers, though his up-and-down success ratio is better than most.

"With sand shots, when you are close to the green, your swing should be more upright, that is like your driver swing. Aim an inch behind the ball, and you must follow through. Trust yourself, be more deliberate. You can't be quick.

"For long bunker shots, remember you must hit the ball first and follow through high."

We can't all play like Zar (though on rare occasions I do beat him), but we can borrow from his practice advice. He offered a few final tidbits.

"Practice with specific shots in mind. You can't just go on the range and hit balls. Have a plan for that day, an objective.

"When you do practice, your grip must always be light. Do not use a death grip. The tighter you grip the club, the less success you'll see because your muscles won't release through the shot. I read about an Olympic rifle shooter who said the more tense his hand is, the less accurate his shot. Too much hand tension is no good. Golf is the same. If your fingers are too tight, your hands won't release through the shot.

"With all shots, look at the ball throughout the shot.

"And always trust yourself."

CHAPTER 15

Hooking, slicing, chunking, and the yips

Nobody loves worm burners, the funky shots that come off the clubface low and fail to get more than a few inches off the ground.

Loathed though they are, worm burners can turn out okay. They are in the class of shots that result in golfers finding their balls and hitting them again. Worm burners may not look pretty, but they can travel one hundred yards or more and leave the golfer with a fair shot at the green.

The variety of failed shots a golfer might strike is as long as the game's history. For hundreds of years, golfers have hooked, sliced, chunked, yipped, shanked, yanked, double-crossed, pulled, whiffed, thinned, bladed, cut, topped, and whatever else might happen accidentally when the face of a club imperfectly finds the surface of a golf ball.

You name it, it's happened. And it's happened to all of us. Even Tiger Woods. Granted, bad shots are rare among professional and high-ranking amateur golfers. They are rare, but they do happen.

I was at a Champions Tour tournament in Naples, Florida, recently, and a fan in the gallery quipped, "I haven't seen any worm burners yet today." He sounded as though he half expected a worm burner.

Elsewhere in *The Common Golfer*, we explore many of the nuances that help to define the game and its hold on its players. We can understand the swing, the ball, the clubs, the turf, and all the myriad of variables that can come together at any given moment.

With so many things that can go wrong on the course, who can blame the golfer who would rather be fishing?

But the fact is, the majority of people who take clubs and balls to first tees around the world are as likely as not to make mistakes on many, if not most, of their golf shots. Mistakes happen. Too often, for many of us.

Wise Irish American Murphy told us, "Anything that can go wrong, will go wrong."

I don't know whether Murphy was a golfer, but his immutable law certainly does apply to those who play the game.

Because balls are round, club faces are flat, and no two swing paths are the same, the odds are high that a slightly imperfect strike will rocket a ball off-line.

Truth is, if bad shots weren't part of our repertoire, would golf be even half as fun? Bear with me as I explain.

Hooks, slices, shanks, and their ilk give us reasons to scold ourselves. And who doesn't need a good scolding now and then?

When your buddy scalds a chip across the green, do you suggest he keep his head down next time? Who can resist stating the obvious when the obvious might jab a little needle?

One day I got a step back and glare from a friend to whom I delivered the encouraging words "get it close" as he lined up a three-foot putt to win the hole. The others chuckled. Who doesn't love a good laugh?

Ballbusting would not be much fun in golf foursomes if we had no hooks, slices, chunks, and missed putts to fuel sarcasm. We would have no time for trash-talking if our buddies never bladed a chip, pulled a wedge, or topped a tee shot into the lake twenty-five feet in front of the tee box. Citing bad shots is as old as the game itself. Somebody sometime long ago thought it would be fun to tease the man whose drive failed to pass the ladies' tee with the challenge not to be mentioned in mixed company. Nobody wants to see that.

If every shot were perfect, what fun would the game really be? I am not a one-trick pony. I also love bass fishing. When I'm not golfing, I tow my boat to a lake and go fishing. Or rather, do I golf on days when I'm not fishing? It's both, I guess. I love fishing and I love golfing, and I frame each game with the same outlook. If every golf shot were perfect, what's left to improve? If I caught a fish on every cast, what remains to be accomplished?

So merrily I go to the golf course, fulfilling my obligation to keep the game interesting, myself humble, and my friends in stitches. I hook, I slice, I chunk, and I yip—and I drive home with smug satisfaction that I am not alone in my failures. Misery loves company, right?

CHAPTER 16
Luck of the draw

Four hours is not a long time, but it can be an eternity when you're paired with a bad apple.

Every golfer's nightmare is discovering a jerk, knucklehead, or loudmouth is waiting on the tee for you. Or worse, he's sharing your cart. If escape is impossible, the next 240 minutes could very well be hell on earth.

You do have choices, however awkward they might be. One option is to grin and bear it. Another is to pull the plug, feign injury or illness, and retreat to the parking lot or grille room.

I suppose the sporting thing is to play your game with as little notice of the antics of the annoying golfer as possible. You can always establish ground rules—"Don't talk to me and I won't talk to you"—but that is rather obvious evidence of your disdain, so it could be ugly in its own right. It begs for a wisecrack response and perhaps more. I've never seen a shoving match on the golf course, but I am certain they do break out.

My golf experiences do include foursomes composed of people with whom I have differences, sometimes even uncomfortable differences. I've opted for the grin-and-bear-it attitude, and things worked out fine.

Politics and sports can be sources of friction. On the golf course, the job, the lake, the tavern, or wherever, I try to remind myself that no matter what I think, it really doesn't need to match up with the other golfer, coworker, angler, or whomever.

If we learn we are like-minded about politics and baseball teams, four hours on the golf course can breeze by in a blur. If we disagree, we can only endure the round by changing the subject—quickly.

Truth is, nobody needs to care about presidential elections, taxes, foreign policy, tariffs, or pennant races once you get to the first tee. Whether you are a conservative, liberal, or middle of the roadster plays no role in getting the ball down the fairway and into the hole.

A golf course is no place for the airing of grievances, but I know golfers who complain from their first swing to their final putt. Interestingly, the complainers do not restrict their disdain to one or two subjects.

Politics and sports are not the only friction points. Consider gender and pace of play.

I know men who would rather go home than discover that the foursome going out before them is a group of ladies. Whether you are a man or a woman or not quite sure, you are no more or less likely to play at a brisk pace. I know male foursomes that plod like land tortoises and female foursomes that disappear out of sight and finish a half hour ahead of my group.

What's more, I know women who play slow, men who are loudmouths, and course rangers who can be more annoying than a swarm of mosquitos on a hot, humid evening.

Who cares? Really.

Your four hours on the golf course—okay, maybe five—are your time to put your focus singularly on the next shot you must hit. One of my personal truisms is that an angry golfer cannot play well. I am guilty of letting my disgust of bad shots, slow play, and bad apple foursomes boil over in my head. If I can blot them out of my thinking, I stand a better chance of making the next shot pay off.

If you don't care about your score, then perhaps your reason to be out there is to relax and soak up some vitamin D. Forget about the rummies out there and your 401(k) and enjoy the moments. You'll have lots of opportunities to vent your frustrations after the clubs are back in your garage.

If, on the other hand, you cannot blot out those who instigate your anger, then it may be time to consider pickleball as your game. There, at least, you can paddle your foes.

CHAPTER 17

To compete or not

Keeping score is one thing. Golfing to win is quite another. To quote a golfer friend, "There's golf. And then there's tournament golf."

Many golfers are content to enjoy their day on the course with little worry about bad shots, missed putts, lost balls, or final scores. They measure the success of the day by the quality of their player companions, the exchange of compliments, and the moments of laughter. If birdies happen, all the better, but if they don't, that's okay.

Those rounds are more social than competition. They have their place in the overall scheme of things in worlds where winning is not important. Another friend, Ted Suffolk, recalled the term coined by a playing companion, "sgolf." It differentiates the social game from golf itself.

"Sgolf is going out with friends and having a nice conversation, enjoying the course you're playing and what's going on around you," Ted said. "In tournaments, it's completely different. You think only about the next shot. You practice beforehand. You try to get your mind in a competitive mode, and hopefully it stays there.

But winning is the name of the game for golfers who thrive on competition. They go to the course with the intent to conquer their foes, hole every shot, and count their winnings.

Come tournament day, the whole field of golfers is happy before the first tee, bubbly even. By the end of the round, the mood is mostly subdued. Only one golfer or one team is overjoyed. Most everyone else is suffering from bad cases of the what ifs. What if I hadn't chunked that 7-iron? What if that chip had not ricocheted off the stick? What if that putt hadn't rimmed out?

Competition golf matters from the first tee to the final green. Matches are often won or lost because of one stroke that miraculously succeeds or unfortunately fails. Professional tournaments are frequently decided by one stroke over three or four days of play.

Professional or amateur, woman or man, young or old, the competition golfer brings keener senses and sharper focus. Anything other than what is required for the next shot becomes irrelevant.

Playing winning golf is what matters, even though the actual score is relative. In many tournaments, the lowest gross score doesn't necessarily take first prize. Competition is handicapped to even the game for the scratch golfer and the eighteen handicapper.

The difference between a 70 and an 80 is obviously ten strokes. The 70 golfer swung the club ten fewer times than the 80 golfer. Ten times over the span of four hours. It hardly seems significant in the overall scheme of things. The 80 represents just a bit more than two more swings per hour. Hardly a big deal, right? Yet the 70 golfer will be telling anyone who will listen about his or her success, while the 80 golfer will be whimpering about the round that got away.

As I noted above, there's golf, and then there is tournament golf.

Golfing friend Dave Newcomb plays two kinds of golf. He takes the same clubs to both games, mind you, and goes after the ball with the instinctive swing he learned many decades ago as a youngster playing hockey in Quebec. He hits the ball solidly, and his score is lower than his age way more often than most of us will ever experience.

"Social golf is bad for my game," said Dave recently as we rode to our second shots on the ninth fairway during a team golf game. He was doing some arithmetic in his head, and the numbers did not please him. "I've been playing more social golf lately, and it's ruined my competition game."

Right or wrong, Dave's theory is shared by many. Distractions get blamed for many of our failures. Many are like Dave.

Focus, blot out noise, no whispers, no sirens, no horns, no crying babies, no squirrels rustling in the leaves, no helicopters whipping the sky, no bees buzzing around the ball you are about to strike.

Some can tune distractions out. Others cannot. Some swing away and utter wisecracks to offenders. "Don't let my swing interrupt your conversation."

Golf buddy Glenn Gallant is a focus guy. When the score counts, his preshot routine is precise, practiced, and purposeful. Noise from the foursome will result in a stare that says "Silence!" without him uttering a word. Lots of golfers are like Glenn.

Others are as cool as a cucumber, and nothing will distract their attention or put a hitch in their swing—not slamming doors, screeching children, or the green flag at the Indianapolis 500.

Competitive golf gets the juices flowing. For many, razzing and trash-talking is a golf match requisite. Golf pal Jim Zarlenga and friendly rival Paul Pirko are champions—in ballbusting. Both are good players, but the daily winner is the one who gets in the most zingers over his four hours of trading barbs and slinging insults. It's all part of the fun of course.

Competition comes in many forms. For the masses, competitive golf is the game they watch on television, professional golfers going toe to toe as individuals and sometimes as teams. Many golf competitors started as children and advanced to whatever level they ultimately achieve.

Adults who do not become accomplished players are not without competitive outlets. Any golfer who is looking to test their game against others can find opportunities at every golf course. Leagues, charity events, local opens, and even clubhouse skins games are tests where the golfer can put up some cash and shoot for the other players' bucks.

Many golfers cannot fathom playing golf without a few dollars on the line. Others cringe at the thought of actually having to worry whether a failed shot might take money from their pocket.

To compete or not to compete? That is the question. Whether you play for one dollar or a thousand dollars, the winner takes bragging rights home to savor until the next time the money goes on the line.

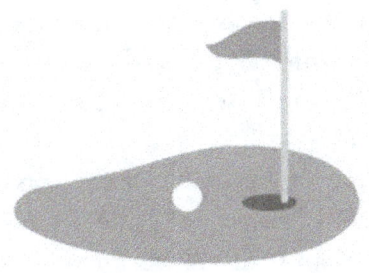

CHAPTER 18

"The Greatest" is gross

Claiming superlatives can be a tricky exercise. Somebody can surpass your claim with a triumphant "uh-huh!" and send you back to the drawing board to try another time.

But two golfers in Youngstown, Ohio, weighed the risks and took the plunge anyway. They noodled up a tournament and titled it The Greatest.

Tall claim? Maybe, but sixteen years later, The Greatest Golfer Youngstown is showing no signs of surrendering its self-proclaimed crown.

Ted Suffolk was the assistant general manager of Youngstown's daily newspaper, *The Vindicator*, and Todd Franko the newly arrived editor when, during a round of golf in 2010, they wondered out loud about the feasibility of holding a community-wide golf tournament. Suffolk and Franko mulled it over, conceived the format, pitched it to golf courses and club pros, secured sponsors, and promoted it to the hilt.

"The Greatest," as they unabashedly nicknamed their baby, was an immediate hit with local amateurs. It continues to thrive and today attracts a large field of men and women who tee it up with high hopes of staking their own claim, knowing nobody can deny them the title of The Greatest if they win.

Suffolk and Franko tried to differentiate their event from the league and country club play with which most of the region's golfers are familiar. "Leagues can be as competitive as hell, which is great, but there really aren't a lot of open events like The Greatest Golfer," said Suffolk, who in his heyday played to a 3.2 index.

The Greatest is gross—a gross-score tournament, that is—divided into divisions for golfers from scratch to the sky's the limit. Entrants can play in men's, women's, youth, senior, and supersenior divisions with players of similar handicap.

A three-day event drawing hundreds of entrants, The Greatest Golfer is contested on a number of private and premium public courses in the Youngstown area. Franko and Suffolk work year-round to secure venues, sponsors, and other details that have propelled the tournament through sixteen years.

"We started with a blank sheet of paper and brought in Dennis Miller [former US Open qualifier and Mill Creek Golf Course pro] and John Diana [former Trumbull Country Club pro] and then got Ed Muransky [owner of The Lake Club and former Los Angeles Raider] and Mike Ferranti [former Lake Club pro] involved. We put the final rounds at the Lake Club, and it was a great success," Suffolk said.

Great competition is the hallmark of the tournament, Franko said. "Certainly the competition is there," he said. "Through the history of The Greatest, we've seen how the players enjoy the competition against each other. I guess what is surprising about it really is more than the competition itself. The players test themselves in different situations than they experience in their Wednesday night league. They compete against thirty to sixty players in their division, and they see those thirty to sixty people as their community. We see camaraderie and players putting themselves to the test. 'How can I do against them?'

"It's one thing to compete over eighteen holes, but having to play at their highest level over three days, they get a chance to see themselves like the guys they see on TV. So seeing them compete against themselves is probably the biggest surprise with The Greatest. Don't get me wrong, some of our playoffs have been epic, but in the end it is often mostly about the players simply competing against themselves, trying to put together their best rounds for their own satisfaction," Franko said.

He noted the tournament is a mental test of competing over four hours for three days with no coaches and no gimmes and players watching every move of their competitors and making sure every putt is holed so there's no monkey business. What's more, the event has its fair share of ballbusting.

The Lake Club is the venue for the final
round of The Greatest Golfer.

"One year, we had a player who shot great out of the chute on day one," Franko said. "Then, on day two we saw he was getting ribbed by his fellow players. He was a high-strung individual. One ballbuster came by and said, 'I'm not worried about your 77 yesterday because you're going to shoot 94 today.' And sure enough, he did. He played himself right out of the tournament."

The Greatest Golfer is like life itself, complete with hijinks and human emotions. "It's like in society, life, and nature. Another thing is the players don't always get along with each other. Some can get really upset; others just shrug their shoulders. We see all kinds of behavior," Franko said.

"Some have noncollegial experiences, but they take it all in stride. One guy a year or so ago did not like the casual nature of his playing partners. They were talking too much and laughing, so after ten holes, he just walked off," he said.

Franko said it also is interesting that the appetite for competition among the ten-, fifteen-, and twenty-handicap golfers is just as keen as it is among the low handicappers.

"Over the history of The Greatest, some of our best competitors are not the scratch players, but the highest division, twenty to twenty-five handicaps. The way those guys prepare is amazing. One guy even buys three new outfits every year just for our tournament. It's great to see their spirit and competitive drive."

Suffolk said another fun aspect of the event is the junior competition and the growth and maturation of the young players. "Over the sixteen years, we've watched them develop into wonderful kids and go on to play in college and return to play in the adult divisions."

The Greatest, like golf itself, looks to be a fixture for the long haul among those who want to test their skills against the best or simply beat their own personal goals.

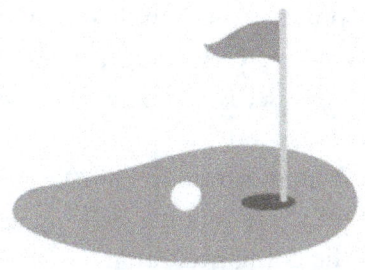

CHAPTER 19

Match play is not for the timid

Golf is always a personal test, player against the field, the course itself, and the shot next to be hit. The game digs into the grit of the people swinging their clubs in competition, that grit often being the deciding factor in winning or losing against competitors with similar skills and talents.

Grit is a factor in stroke play, but it really plays large in match play, which I believe is the ultimate test of the golfer. The ultimate, yes, and as such, it is not for the weak or timid. Indeed, talent alone is not enough to win in a game where the victor is the one who not only succeeds shot after shot and putt after putt but who also reaches deep inside and grabs a handful of grit that delivers traction when the game is on the line.

Match play, for those who are unfamiliar with the game, is golfer versus golfer. Your total score is relatively unimportant in match play because each hole is its own contest. If your score on Number 1, for example, is 5 and your opponent's is 6, you win the hole and go "one up" in the match. And so on. The winner of the match is the golfer who wins the most holes.

I really like match play. I can blow up on a hole, shrug it off, and simply pick up and move on. Every hole presents a fresh opportunity to win. It's fun and challenging. It's also fraught with tension.

So it was that recent day when I teed up in my match in our Florida club's annual President's Cup. It is a single elimination bracket tournament contested during winter's high season. Players move on in the bracket

65

after dispatching their opponents in handicapped matches.

As fate would have it, my match was against good friend Duffy Lynch. Friend versus friend, I suppose, is to be expected in a golf club setting where everybody knows everybody.

I never let on (so don't mention this to him), but I was nervous about going toe to toe with Duffy. He hits the ball longer than I hit it and is known to go low when the going gets tough.

Duffy is a wisecracking Rhode Islander who, now past age seventy, has reverted to his rowdy younger days with a four-inch ponytail sprouting from the back of his cap. It adds to the Duffy mystique, as do the F bombs and other colorful expressions that pepper his conversations. As his friends acknowledge, "That's Duffy."

Under his confident veneer, however, Duffy is like all of us common golfers. A topped tee shot or a chunked iron can crack confidence quicker than an omelet chef opening eggs at his prep station. My prematch thoughts focused not so much on the booming drives he might unleash as on the pushed slices I imagined he might carve out of bounds. So it was with a dose of confidence of my own that I shook hands with my opponent friend, wished him good luck, and proceeded to the first tee.

Our golf club sends out President's Cup matches as twosomes, so it was just Duffy and me in the cart when we arrived at the first tee. The course was full of foursomes in front of us, so the next four hours were going to offer plenty of time to soak in success and anguish over failures. Both of us would ride high and sink low. We would overthink, overreact, and over everything that enters the fragile zone between our respective ears.

Our match began dead even. Our handicaps were identical, so neither took a stroke advantage to the first tee. We understood the outcome was not going to boil down to an excuse, a handicap differential.

Things started well for me. I won the tricky first hole and daunting second. Going two up put a bounce in my steps as I walked to the third tee, but a moment later I was sulking over the dunking of my drive. Duffy won that hole, tightening the match and stealing whatever momentum I imagined was on my side of the cart.

Momentum is critical. When it's flowing your way, it is like you're surfing a tsunami. When it's on the other guy's side, it's like you're stuck in a snowdrift in the path of an onrushing avalanche.

I went back to two up after Hole 10, feeling pretty frisky. Even my Hole 11 snap-hooked tee shot, which splashed in a lake, didn't dampen my enthusiasm. My confidence was buoyed when Duffy pushed his tee ball out of bounds and followed that with a slice that also went OB. Usually able to dust off mistakes with expletive-laden wisecracks, Duffy was fuming.

My brain went into overdrive. Thoughts raced. How could I lose this hole? I'm on the verge of going three up!

Then, things turned south for me. I shall spare you the tragic details, but suffice to say Duffy won the hole with a four-over-par 8. That is about as unthinkable as your twelve-year-old Little Leaguer pitching in

Author Jack Wollitz splits the prize pot with
match play teammate Dave Newcomb.

the World Series.

Of course, the avalanche swept over me, and I lost the next two holes. But Duffy pushed his Hole 14 tee shot OB, and I carded a par to stop the bleeding. The tourniquet held, and I won 16 to go one up with two to play. He nipped me on 17, and we arrived at 18 all square.

People talk about "the golf gods," the supposedly fair overseers who mete out justice on the course. They were no doubt smiling about the day's turns of events, as two players with identical handicaps rode highs and survived lows to stand even on the final hole.

Nerves? Maybe. But we both arrived within a chip of the eighteenth flag in two shots. Duffy knocked his third shot to the center of the green. I flubbed the third, put it on in four, and two putted to lose.

"Congratulations, Duffy." They are the words that must be said. But we both knew what had just transpired. Nobody won the match. One of us lost it.

He earned the opportunity to advance to the next rung on the bracket. He will tee off versus Audie, our club's scratch golfer. One may win that match or one may lose it. Either way, someone will advance to the next round, and the tournament will play on.

That's match play, survival of the fittest in a game not recommended for the faint of heart.

CHAPTER 20

A course for a cause

A spread of hills and dales, grass and trees sprawls to the south of US 30 in eastern Stark County, Ohio. It is a golf course in a county chock-full of golf courses, but with a history so distinctive that it can rightfully be declared an American landmark, even an American treasure.

William J. Powell built that golf course because when he returned home after his World War II military service, he found no place that welcomed him to golf. He felt the sting, saw the need, and jumped into action. Thus was born Clearview Golf Club, a course in East Canton, Ohio, where every golfer was welcome, regardless of their skin color.

Powell was a trailblazer. An Ohio Historical Marker chronicles his accomplishment: "Golfer and World War II veteran William J. Powell, excluded from playing on many American golf courses because of his race, overcame the indignity of discrimination by creating his own course. Hand built in two years and first nine opened in 1948, Clearview Golf Club is the first golf course in the United States designed, built, and owned by an African American. Second nine opened in 1978. The acclaimed course harmonizes with the landscape and bears many design elements of traditional courses. A triumph of perseverance over discrimination, Clearview represents the historic postwar era when athletes first broke the 'color line' in American sports."

Bill's daughter Renee Powell is also a trailblazer. She began swinging a golf club at age three and soon learned to excel. She was the second African American woman to compete on the LPGA tour, after Althea Gibson, and played in more than 250 tournaments around the world while also finding time for a USO tour of Vietnam. She made history when she became the first woman head professional at the private Silvermere Golf Club in the United Kingdom. She and her family achieved many other significant accomplishments.

She said her father's vision extended beyond simply building a golf course.

"He was about creating opportunities," Renee said. "He built this golf course despite discrimination and racism. In England and Scotland, he was able to golf everywhere. Here, he couldn't do that. Black soldiers came home and didn't even have GI loans and benefits. They weren't welcome even at public courses. He tried to create opportunities.

"He believed in opportunities for all people. For example, women weren't welcome on courses. Kids weren't welcome. He came from Minerva, where there was only one black family in town. Clearview wasn't just for black people. It is for everyone, regardless of the color of your skin, your hair, or your eyes, or your religion."

Following her LPGA Tour career, Renee continued her dedication to diversifying golf and extending the mission of her father to make golf accessible to all. She's received numerous honors for her work, including a building dedicated in her name at the University of St. Andrews in Scotland in 2018. In 2015, she became one of only two American women initially gaining honorary membership into the Royal and Ancient Golf Club in St. Andrews. In 2008, she was the third American and only woman golfer to receive an honorary degree from the University of St. Andrews. She also is a board member emeritus of the Pro Football Hall of Fame. Her namesake Renee Powell Cup is awarded annually to the winner of the National Women's Collegiate Golf Championship.

All of that and so much more is a testimony to the inspiration of Bill Powell. From those hundred acres of woods and meadows sprouted a movement that is as important today as it was just after World War II.

Even its name is significant.

"From up on the hill, he had a clear view. My dad was an intelligent man, and he had a clear view of the future of things," Renee said.

"If not for Clearview, I wouldn't have played golf. My dad put a golf club in my hand when I was three. I still have that club. I got serious around age ten and competed at age twelve."

Her first event was in a UGA tournament in Cleveland. The United Golfers Association had been formed because there were no places for blacks to play tournaments.

"Blacks were allowed to play only a few courses back then, like Senaca and Highland in Cleveland and South Park and North Park in Pittsburgh. Back then, golf was so prejudiced, racist, so that's why the UGA was established," Renee said.

"I played in the UGA at Seneca. My dad put me in the tournament in Cleveland in the women's division, not the kids' division. The women I played with were the same age as my parents, and they didn't want a

Retired LPGA tour pro Renee Powell with Barb Wollitz. Renee today operates Clearview Golf Club, built by her father, William Powell.

kid to beat them, so they weren't very nice to me. I won the B Division. After that, the women became my biggest fans over the years. That was my first tournament. Dad always said, 'Once you get them one down, get them two down, and when you get them two down, get them three down.'"

Clearview has been and will continue to be a family operation. Renee's brother Larry has worked there since he was eight years old and today is the superintendent. Her mother, Marcella, founded what now is the longest-running ladies golf league in Stark County, Ohio.

The Powells completed a major irrigation system installation in 2025 and remain dedicated to service, including the mission of the Clearview Legacy Foundation for Education, Preservation, and Turfgrass Research.

The "education" mission is to use golf as a tool to assist young people and seniors, minorities, people with troubles, women military veterans, and people with physical and mental challenges. It includes golf programs and workshops to jump-start young women in the game.

The "preservation" efforts include adding an education and archival facility to teach the game and its history.

"Turfgrass research" sprang from the fact Clearview for most of its history lacked an automatic sprinkler system. The Powells worked hard to keep the grass growing during hot, dry Ohio summers. Larry Powell developed practices involving slow-release fertilizers and testing different grasses to determine the most resilient varieties.

"Larry has been involved much more than me. I left here in 1965 and came back in 1994. He's been here all along. It's always been a family thing."

That "family thing" has not gone unnoticed. The Powells were named the National Golf Foundation Jack Nicklaus Golf Family of the Year in 1992. Bill Powell received the PGA of America Distinguished Service Award in 2009 and was inducted into the National Black Golf Hall of Fame in 1996 and the PGA of America Hall of Fame in the class of 2013. The family also was the recipient of the 2019 Old Tom Morris Award by the Golf Course Superintendents Association of America.

Despite the accomplishments and accolades, the path hasn't been without resistance. When asked to name a significant moment during her career, Renee did not hesitate to answer, "The first time I ever received a threat letter on my life—for playing golf in my own country."

She also found time to coach her local high school girls' golf team and is particularly proud to share a very important honor bestowed on her when East Canton High School senior and golfer Mia Steigerwald invited her to the National Honor Society induction. "The students spoke about their 'person,' and I was her person. It really is nice. I'm such a homebody, really. My life has taken me around the world, so I appreciate it when I'm able to be home."

Renee, Larry, and Clearview itself are extending the legacy of Bill Powell.

"Dad's legacy is that golf is for everyone. My role? I guess it's a little bit of everything. I'm a golf professional. I love playing the game of golf and understanding why certain things are important and how everybody can make positive changes in society if they chose to. My whole family has worked hard and made sacrifices. I don't feel I had a choice not to preserve this legacy."

Bill Powell's own words are showcased on a wall-size tribute to Clearview Golf Club at a travelers' rest area on Interstate 76 in Ohio. The words are ones he spoke frequently and sincerely.

"The only color that matters is the color of the greens."

The significance of Clearview Golf Club is celebrated in a roadside display on Ohio's Interstate 76.

Clubs and balls and other stuff we crave

Punsters proudly proclaim, "You can't play golf without balls," and laugh at their own joke even as women roll their eyes.

While boys will be boys, the truth is equipment is pretty important in the game of golf, and 99.3 percent of its players own their clubs and balls (okay, I made up that percentage, but I would think it's a pretty good guess).

Clubs and balls are essential, but they are chosen by their owners under different criteria. Balls are purchased by the dozen with full knowledge that while they are not necessarily disposable, it is highly unlikely that you'll own that dozen for more than a few weeks. They cost anywhere from a dollar each to four bucks and more, depending on the brand you select based on performance and prestige.

One thing about golf balls: you don't always get what you pay for. Unless you are a low handicapper, if you buy a $48-per-dozen box of balls, you will not be assured of better scores than the $12-a-dozen balls at Walmart. What's more, both brands will sink like rocks to the bottom of the lake and rocket off into the woods at the speed of light.

Buying balls can be a grab-and-go endeavor. You can stop on the way to the golf course and restock your bag when you're running low. You have many other options of course, but the point is shopping is not a big deal.

Selecting golf clubs, on the other hand, is a lot more complicated. You will be investing hundreds, even thousands, of dollars, and you will be hoping to get at least several years' use. Buying clubs is a very personal endeavor, with many considerations. You can buy them off the floor at a retailer or order online or through your golf club's pro shop. Choosy golfers will opt for a proper fitting under the watchful eye of a professional trained to match your swing and your capabilities with the right clubs, shafts, and loft and lie.

Clubs can be bewildering for beginners. It's not unlike a newcomer going to buy a car in a town with twenty car dealers. Where do you even begin?

Beginners bring a perspective, an innocence even, that veteran golfers might find quaint. I learned this many years ago when a freshman on my wife Barb's high school golf team asked, "Do we need our own golf clubs?" Another player admitted her clubs were a set claimed from a neighbor's trash put out for the next day's collection.

From the neophyte with hand-me-down equipment to the scratch golfer who buys a new $599 driver every spring, golfers use a range of golf clubs as broad as the ocean. I've seen it all, I suppose, though I'm familiar only with my tiny fraction of the wide world of golfers.

I have played with people toting the venerable "Sunday bag" with a twenty-five-year-old driver, a dented fairway metal, 3-irons, a spoon-shaped sand wedge, and a putter that he probably inherited from his grandfather. I also have played with a fellow who admitted he had just plunked down $3,000 for his sparkling new clubs and shushed me to not let his wife overhear us discussing the total cost.

So many options. Graphite or steel? Length? Flex? And that's just shafts. What about grips? How about irons' loft and lie? And hybrids bring a completely different set of options into play.

All of that is important of course. The better the equipment, the better the score, yes? Sure, premium clubs feel good, perform well, and make their owners proud, so it stands to reason that a par round or sub-80 for bogey golfers is more likely to happen than if they are swinging bargain-basement sticks.

Here's a hard truth, however. Thirty years ago, I went through a Saturday evening shopping phase, buying new putters on a whim. I'm not talking about pro shop recommendations. Rather, they were impulse buys from the putter rack at Walmart. Most of them stickered at $9.98.

I'd drop my new find in my bag Sunday morning, sink a few putts, and collect skins that covered my ten-buck investments.

As important as golf clubs are, I am amazed by many golfers' tolerance for grips in poor condition. More times than I can count I have picked up playing partners' wedges left greenside and marveled at their slick grips. How, I wonder, can they possibly feel good about gripping a surface as slick as an icicle?

As long as we are on the topic of equipment, I must tell you I am amused by the assemblages of brushes dangling from rings attached to friends' golf bags. The two-brush tools are handy—one side with soft bristles and the other with wire to clean the grooves in their clubs' faces. I admire such golfers' preparedness, but the truth is if you need a stiff wire brush to rid your clubs of caked mud, you aren't wiping them nearly often enough.

All manner of accessories are available—and purchased obviously— for golfers who wish to be ready for everything. I see lots of hand-shaped forms for airing out gloves. And beads. I estimate one out of every three women has score-counting beads on her person during her rounds.

Regardless of brand, cost, or sentimental value, all golf balls
sink like rocks.

Some golfers seem to find security in stocking their bags with stuff. You know who they are. They always have a bottle of ibuprofen, bandages, tape, a dozen divot repair tools, extra towels, enough ball markers for every man, woman, and child in their respective clubs, and plastic sandwich bags bulging with tees.

Barb's a tee hoarder. At the conclusion of every round, she plucks the tees from her golf cart and drops them in her golf bag. She periodically has to purge her stash, but not before they number enough to kindle a roaring fire. Anybody got a match?

And then there are the golf ball over achievers, the folks who never leave the starter's stand without three dozen balls. Either they experience a lot of penalty strokes or they just feel ill prepared with only a dozen in the bag. Thinking this through, I'm theorizing they probably are the same people who get nervous when the number of ketchup bottles in the pantry dips below six.

Golf balls make golf bags heavy. Ask the bag-drop player assistants who have to heft them.

Sometimes, of course, players accumulate balls without noticing how many are in their bags. Ball hawking is fair sport for those who frequently play their game on the periphery of our golf courses. If you are always in the middle of the fairway, you are far less likely to discover abandoned Titleists, Bridgestones, TaylorMades, Srixons, and Callaways. No golfer can resist pocketing such treasures, even though our bags are heavy with balls.

Choosy golfers, on the other hand, pass up bargain-priced balls. I do admit, however, that I will pick up el cheapo balls if they are colorful. They are like Easter eggs hiding in the bushes, irresistible for sure. Chartreuse, orange, and pink balls come in handy sometimes, if for no other purpose than to share with players who prefer them. Nothing says friendship like greeting with gifts.

Clubs, balls, tools, and gadgets all add up to a golfer's very own personalization of the game. Whether they subtract strokes is only one factor. But if they bring satisfaction, that is reason enough to have them on game day.

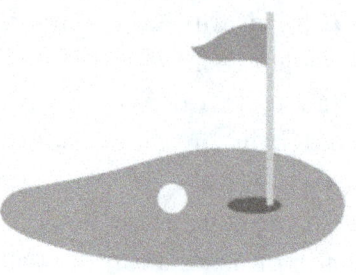

CHAPTER 22

Technology and the common golfer

In the fitness room of the home of my daughter and her husband in Columbus, Ohio, stands a time machine of sorts, a device that can transport a golfer to another land whenever they want. The machine has a brain, eyes, and other sensors. It sees, reads, and interprets the results of a golf swing and then displays the outcome in a visual real enough to enable the imaginative golfer to feel the warmth of the sun, the smell of the grass, and the thrill of a well-struck shot.

Simulators are popping up everywhere—from golf courses to entertainment centers to the homes of golfers who want to hone their game in rain, snow, or sunshine, all without driving out to the driving range. They are the tip of the iceberg that technology has produced, which is high-performance products for golfers, including us common golfers who can beg, borrow, and buy just about anything the tour professional might be using.

Simply put, the stuff at our disposal today was a pipe dream in the heydays of our fathers and mothers. Today's golf balls, clubs, laser range finders, and golf cart GPS bring great advantages to players in distance, accuracy, and pure fun.

The popularity of simulator golf has grown since the first machines were developed in the 1970s. Entertainment centers featuring simulators are popping up everywhere. Golf retailers use them to fit clubs for customers. Golf clubs install them to provide golfers with options during inclement weather and to practice between rounds. Golf pros use them to teach their student golfers. And now professional golfers like Tiger Woods and Rory McIlroy have anted up to bring tour-level golf indoors in an arena-style, made-for-TV format enabled by sophisticated simulator technology.

Some see the simulator stimulating the game. The technology enables golfers to play a game that typically spans hundreds of acres within the confines of a closet, albeit a very large closet. All with a realism that grows more intense every time a new version is released.

Today's technology makes balls fly faster and straighter, clubs strike balls sweeter, golfers measure distance instantly and plan shots more accurately. It makes practice more convenient.

So are golfers getting better?

That's a loaded question. I had my doubts, so I turned to technology to do some research about whether today's golfers are better today than, say, forty years ago. I googled the question.

Google served up a 2024 *Golf Digest* article by Drew Powell. Powell had asked the question himself as he pondered the ongoing conversation about whether golf ball performance needed to be rolled back. He cited a *Golf Digest* article in 2024 by Editor Jerry Tarde, who reported on a USGA survey of a quarter million golfers' handicaps, 76 percent men and 24 percent women.

The survey found that in 1983, men's average handicap index was seventeen and women's average index was 31.5. In 2023, men's average dipped to fourteen and women's to twenty-eight. The article goes on to explain the differences then and now regarding formulas and calculations, but the gist is that indeed, common golfers today are several strokes better than those from our parents' generation. The article notes that today's clubs are more forgiving, more hybrids are in play, and we have a larger variety of wedges with various surfaces and bounce.

Powell wrote, "What's more, the golf ball spins less and flies farther today, and off-center strikes no longer dive offline as quickly. . . . All of this is to say what we already know (or think we know), anecdotally: golf today is easier than it was 40 years ago."

The writer goes on to explain that even with the advances in technology resulting in better equipment and convenient practice that provides instant feedback, the game itself is still very difficult.

Something to think about: the game is hard, and new tech stuff is helping us score lower, but should we be playing even better? I think that is difficult to judge.

Technology, in the meantime, will continue to help the game and the golfer. Looking back at what technology has served up today activates some exciting thoughts. What wonders will we experience in the years to come?

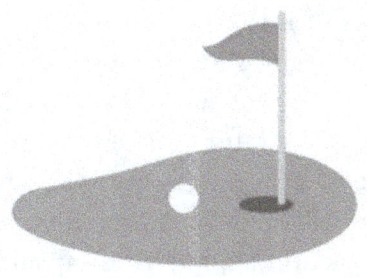

CHAPTER 23

I should have paid attention in college physics

He says it is meditation. But it would seem to be more of an obsession. Plus he thinks about the game much differently than most common golfers.

He is Chris Loizides. He came to golf relatively late in the game.

"I was an engineer and kind of an introvert," he said, looking back and providing clues about how golf hacked its way into his soul.

"I started playing golf at age fifty-seven because I was visiting a friend who had just purchased a home on a golf course. I had never played golf. It seemed dumb to me. You hit a ball, find the ball and hit it again, hope to find it, and hit it again.

"It just seemed dumb. But then I found if you visualized faces on those balls, hitting them could be interesting. In a week, I was addicted." (Note to psychiatrist: I guess that is one way to vent some steam.)

Loizides said golf was a game changer for him. "I started to see golf like meditation. I was an introvert, and I realized you have to be willing to play with people you don't know. The socialization aspect of golf is good."

Visualizing faces was not his only fixation on golf balls.

"As I played, I would find golf balls lost by others and started to see that two balls always went further and stopped quicker," he said. His engineering instincts fed his curiosity about golf ball flight. "I wanted to know everything about the ball and the clubs."

Loizides's curiosity led to deep study involving his own testing and charting information he's gained empirically and in fully equipped golf simulators.

"I study all aspects of golf from an engineer's perspective. I have studied wedges and the advantages of various grinds and bounce. I have studied the handicap system. You should see the reaction I get from guys when they bitch about their index and handicap and I recite the formula and show them why it costs two strokes to move to the Number 3 tees. I just like to understand.

"However, it is frustrating to understand all this but not be able to play well." Ah, that oft-cited lament of the common golfer. Loizides's handicap index is twenty-one.

Loizides could have relied on previously conducted ball testing, but his engineering mind kicked in, and he formulated his own study. I asked him to summarize his deep dive into golf balls, which he chronicled in a report suited for presentation at a scientific conference.

"Say I have found a ball, hit it, and it takes off like a shot from a cannon. Why? There are over one thousand golf balls to pick from. What are the differences? Most guys we play with think the ball makes no difference. I disagree.

"When I started my quest, I took seven sleeves of different golf balls to the simulator, and the pro brought a Pro V and a Pro V1x. I hit the balls many times, recording the performance of each with a driver and a 7-iron."

Loizides said he found dramatic differences in length, the biggest coming off the driver.

"Some balls were as much as twenty yards longer. But the longer balls were also prone to fade or slice a bit more or in some cases a lot more. The culprit was side spin, which the simulator could measure.

"So, do you want a drive of two hundred yards in the rough, woods, or water? Or do you want a drive of 185 to 190 yards in the fairway?"

The results of Loizides's ball test highlighted more than length differentials. His data helped him understand how balls react on approach shots, including how much spin was generated.

"Do you want the ball to stop? I tested with wedges and a 9-iron. The cheap two-piece balls that may go long and straight do not stop well when hit from inside 110 yards. After my ball tests I ended up using a Wilson ball and dropped my index significantly. I also use a different ball for shorter par threes than I do for longer holes based on spin performance."

The engineer in him grinned. "I find golf balls and the physics of golf fascinating."

No kidding?

"Golf has a lot of puzzling physics, like you have to hit down to make it go up."

One gets the sense Loizides's curiosity will not cool soon. "Every time I fix something, something else breaks," he said.

Beyond his pursuit of evidence and utter fascination with physics and ball dynamics, Loizides is the poster child for the common golfer.

"I had a very difficult job as director of information technology for a federally funded research and development company with 103 offices around the world, meaning we had stuff going on twenty-four seven.

"The job was very stressful. I went to the gym at five every morning just to burn off stress. However, I found that playing golf, even bad golf, reduced the impact of stress. Why? As it turns out, to play golf you must focus, pay complete attention to what you are doing, and eliminate spurious BS and interruptions.

"So in a sense, if you really are playing golf, not just swinging the club, you are completely immersed. When the round is over, you are in a sense as refreshed as you are after meditation."

He has no qualms about revealing his idiosyncrasies.

"I always try to be the first one to tee off on every hole. Why? Because I am a Type A personality from Boston, and I am inpatient and always in a hurry. But that is just one part of it. I have found that if I follow someone who hits a really good shot, I want to hit it as long or longer. In your mind, you are competing against the other golfers. You may be in a match, but you are really competing against the golf course.

"If you play tennis, you have to return a ball hit to you by an opponent. You actually have to beat the opponent. In basketball, you have to score, but you also have to stop the opponent from scoring. . . . In golf, you are only comparing scores. Your opponent takes no direct action to impede you.

"So if you change your mindset from 'I am competing against Jack' to 'I am competing against Glen Eagle hole Number 9,' it changes your thinking and, I believe, your behavior."

He said it is important to acknowledge other golfers have no real influence over you unless you let them.

"There will be times when the other players' performance may influence you because of the score. But in general, playing the course gives you a better chance of shooting a better score than trying to beat your opponent shot by shot.

Inevitably for Loizides, the conversation will come back to the balls. He offered one more revelation.

"My latest discovery is Maxfli Tour X, a four-piece cast urethane ball we get on sale for twenty-five dollars per dozen. It performs as well as the previous version Pro V1 for less than half the price."

He gets a kick out of being right.

"Three people who told me in a rather harsh manner that the ball does not make a difference have purchased many dozens of these balls. One guy was so embarrassed that it took him ten days to tell me he liked them so much after trying one that he went to Golf Galaxy and bought four dozen!"

CHAPTER 24

Inside the ropes: up close with the greatest golfers on the planet

Golf fans have the rarest of opportunities to get up close and personal with the professionals in their sport.

Sports fans dream of sitting with the stars in Major League Baseball dugouts or roaming the bench areas at NFL venues. Basketball fans would love to huddle up with LeBron James or Michael Jordan or even score courtside seats alongside Spike Lee or Jack Nicholson. In most sports, it simply isn't easy to get within earshot of conversations. Rarely are we able to reach out and pat our heroes on their backs.

Professional golf tournaments, on the other hand, put fans up close and personal with the players and their entourages. Fans often get friendly fist bumps as the tour pros pass by, and some even get to jump the ropes and volunteer for jobs important in the conduct of the tournaments.

Standing tall and walking briskly with chins square and scoreboards upright, the standard-bearers in professional golf tournaments are like the signifers for a Roman legion. They declare the identity of the combatants and post their scores for the gallery's edification. It's a great job, which they earn simply by volunteering.

Consider the experiences of Glenn Gallant and Clark Gable (no, not the star of *Gone with the Wind*). They split their year between homes in New England and Naples, Florida, and have as their common denominator stints as standard-bearers for professional golf tournaments at the Ritz Carlton Tiburon course.

Clark has volunteered to serve as standard-bearer in several Chubb Classic PGA Champions Tour events as well as the LPGA's CME Championship. Glenn was a standard-bearer in the 2022 Chubb, enduring long days on his soon-to-be-replaced knee.

"It was worth the effort, for sure, as I drew Bernhard Langer, Retief Goosen and Ernie Els my very first day," Glenn said, recalling the thrill of accompanying the three PGA Hall of Famers as they played their way around Greg Norman's Tiburon Black layout.

Clark said the value of walking with pro golfers is beyond measure. "It's like a three-day golf lesson. It's pretty humbling how far the ladies can hit the ball," he said of his work at the LPGA CME Championship.

Glenn armed himself with technology to measure the moments. "I wore my GPS golf watch so I could know exactly where they were hitting from, the yardage. It was amazing to see a guy hitting a 6-iron 230 yards and bending it around a corner."

Glenn Gallant on the move as the standard-bearer at the PGA Champions Tour Chubb Classic at Tiburon in Naples.

Clark's 2025 marquee golfers included Langer, Alex Čejka, Freddie Jacobson, Tim O'Neal, Mark Walker, and Felipe Aguilar. "I love golf, so it's really fun to be out there with those guys. They are so good."

The job is not just about gawking at the stars.

"When it's windy out there, you really have to hang on to that sign pretty good," Clark said. The physical effort is real. Glenn said, "It's very physical. The sign gets heavy, and you walk about six miles, so you've got to be in pretty good shape. I remember trying to steer the sign to avoid it catching the wind."

Standard-bearers also must be alert to move swiftly, often while changing their scoreboard's numbers on the run.

Glenn recalled the long transit from a tee to the next green at Tiburon. "They shuttled us in carts, and there was only one seat—next to Langer—so I hesitated, and he motioned me to sit next to him. I didn't want to say anything to interrupt his thoughts, but he spoke up and made sure to mention that he appreciated us doing our jobs. That was pretty cool."

Clark said Champions Tour player Scott McCarron reminded him that golf, regardless of one's skills, can be humbling.

Standard-bearers also get the inside scoop on the interaction between caddies and their pros. Their routines quickly become apparent. "They have it down to a science," Clark said. Glenn added, "I wanted to know what they were saying, but I didn't want to get too close. I would check the yardage on my watch, but I didn't want them to catch me eavesdropping."

Both men said standard-bearers can learn how to improve their own game if they pay attention.

"I learned I've got to pay more attention to what I'm doing and slow down, take my time. When you really watch them, you see they're like statues," Clark said.

Glenn added, "To me, the biggest thing is their focus. It was great to watch them dial in. When it was time to shoot, they were really dialed in."

With all of the distractions, the standard-bearers also have to be dialed in.

"The first day, I felt like I was on a stage with a bunch of actors," Glenn said. "I was nervous at first. What should I do? Where should

I stand? But I always tried to make sure the gallery could see my sign. That's why you're out there. I also wanted to make sure I had the right number posted. You really don't want to put up the wrong number!"

Both men talked about the pride inside while bearing the standard. "It was great to wave to friends from our club. It's kind of funny. They were outside the ropes. I was inside. It made me feel important," Glenn said.

"You ARE important," Clark said. "You're on the inside."

Golf fans can get up close with professional stars like Lexi Thompson.

Stars shine bright

Even with the ropes separating the players from the riffraff, we fans still get the opportunity to eavesdrop on the conversations and see the sweat on their brows. Plus we even bump into celebrities.

I'm not easily starstruck. Not to toot my horn, but I have sat with Paul Newman in a car and bumped shoulders with Ernest Borgnine in the pits just before the green flag of the Indianapolis 500. It's still a thrill when a famous person glances my way. It's happened several times at professional golf tournaments.

Fresh from the NBA championship won by the Cleveland Cavaliers, star forward J. R. Smith was inside the ropes at the Bridgestone tournament at Firestone Country Club in Akron. He passed within bumping distance as he ducked under the rope to shortcut to the next tee, his towering and tattooed presence leaving no mistaking his identity or the reason he could dominate on NBA hardwood.

A few years ago at Naples's Tiburon, I spied John O'Hurley, who starred as the eccentric J. Peterman in the *Seinfeld* TV series. He seemed to be trying to blend into the gallery, but his tall stature and distinctive J. Peterman face made it clear we were in the presence of a star.

You never know who we might bump into out there.

CHAPTER 25

Do you mind if I play music?

Here's a question I doubt was ever posed to Bobby Jones: "Do you mind if I play music?"

Of course, Jones's playing days were over long before the proliferation of devices portable enough to bring Beethoven, Pitbull, or the Rolling Stones to our fairways. I do wonder, nevertheless, how Jones, Hogan, Snead, and Whitworth would have responded to a player suggesting some music to make their day brighter.

Truth is, I'm not sure where I stand on golf course music. I have some thoughts. You probably have yours. Who is right?

"Silence is golden," say golfers who insist they cannot succeed unless they can withdraw into a soundproof chamber during their preshot routine.

"Relax," say proponents of music to soothe their nerves.

"Respect," say those who believe music assaults their senses.

"Hell's bells," say some with a shrug, "it doesn't matter."

The matter of music is a can of worms. But assume, for a moment, that music is going to be part of your golf day. What shall we play?

Genre is critical. Shall we go with classical? Rock? Country? Jazz? Bluegrass? Pop? Instrumental? Opera? Hip hop? Maybe a little Herb Alpert and the Tijuana Brass?

The larger question here is this: can a foursome really agree on music? I think the answer is: it depends.

Are you all going to a Taylor Swift concert after your round? Then your music choice is right there in front of you.

Are you teeing it up in Nashville? Tune to Tim McGraw.

Are there alligators in the ponds and crawfish on the menu? Play some bayou fiddle and accordion tunes.

Are you a golf traditionalist? Get in the mood with Celtic music.

Music or not, and if so, what? There are no right or wrong answers. It's a matter of choice and even deciding whether the majority rules. It's important to keep in mind of course that whatever happens, it certainly must not ruin your round.

Here's the thing: It's probably a fact that early golfers sometimes heard music as they trudged the heaths and greens. Though I doubt pipes and mandolins accompanied early foursomes, I do imagine some music rode the sea breezes from nearby villages to gorse-lined fairways.

Music does have meaningful links with golf. Just as baseball has "Take Me Out to the Ball Game," golf has bagpiper performances. They include the famous sunset medleys featuring "Scotland the Brave" along Pebble Beach to the Inn at Spanish Bay.

What is considered good music is in the ears of the listener. Though some cover their ears when the bagpipes inflate, it's a far cry more melodic than Harry Carey singing during the seventh-inning stretch. The pipers' tunes often bring tears, but for me, at least, the tears flow because of too many failed shots.

A distant piper is one thing; a squeaky speaker stuck to a golf cart windshield frame is another. Portable players pose a predicament. The answer might very well be WWBJD? What would Bobby Jones do?

If the tunes get you happily through eighteen holes, turn them on. But if you'd rather swing in silence, then just say no.

CHAPTER 26

My favorite eighteen holes

It is without question that many golfers live in fantasy worlds. We are, after all, convinced tomorrow will bring the best round we've ever played.

Golf is so personal that all of us, every man, woman, and child, sooner or later establish in our own minds where we fit in the overall scheme of things. While many play as though the history of golf began the day they made their first swing, some become convinced they own a piece of the game's heritage. Golf is great that way. It can be whatever we want it to be.

Sports fans are fortunate to have many ways to scratch their fantasy itch. Baseball fans, for instance, often build lists of ballparks they wish to visit. Auto racing buffs travel to legendary racecourses around the world. Tennis people would pay a king's ransom to play Wimbledon. High school football teams dream of the day they will play on the home turf of their favorite college or NFL squads.

Consider golf courses. Talk about your fixings for fantasy. Google says our world is blessed with nearly thirty-nine thousand golf courses. I have been fortunate to have teed up on more than one hundred of them (I list them at the end of this chapter so you can compare with your list.)

Out of more than eighteen hundred golf holes sprinkled across ten states, I have winnowed down a list of holes that make up my fantasy track. After fifty years of trying like hell, I certainly have dug enough divots to qualify as "experienced"— a euphemism for hacker—but, more importantly, I can look back on fond and fun memories to assemble my favorite eighteen.

Walk with me to the first tee.

HOLE 1: Easy is good sometimes in golf. The starting hole at picturesque Beaver Creek Meadows in Columbiana County, Ohio, is just exactly what you want to kickstart your round. It's a straightaway par four, drivable for many, with a receptive flat green protected by a bunker. Take your birdie and smile. If you make a 6, turn around and go home. It's not your day.

HOLE 2: Yeah, a little name-dropping here. I carded a birdie on the second hole at Pebble Beach, a par five for those of us who don't play championship golf. I walked off the second green like I was treading on Cloud Nine.

HOLE 3: The third hole at Pine Lakes in Hubbard, Ohio, is a hundred-yard par three. The shot is to a green well below the tee box, and it can be a bit tricky depending on the wind. The flag is framed by an oak tree looming large to the left of the hole and a covered bridge spanning the creek that runs in front of the green.

HOLE 4: Longleaf, one of the dozens of quality golf courses in Pinehurst, North Carolina, is built for the common golfer, offering seven tee boxes to fit every skill level. The fourth hole is a fine example, setting up anywhere from 89 to 186 yards. It's a delightful par three at whatever distance you choose.

HOLE 5: From Pinehurst, we go a few hours west to the fifth hole at Woodfin Ridge, Inman, South Carolina. It's another par three, but I am okay with an abundance of them. Five at Woodfin Ridge is no cakewalk, however, as it is all uphill to a well-bunkered green. By the way, the snack bar's hot dog is one of the best in golf.

HOLE 6: Jack Nicklaus's signature Old Corkscrew in Lee County, Florida, is a tough track, with the sixth hole challenging all levels of golfers. Tee shots must be long and straight to stand a chance at par.

HOLE 7: The peninsula green on the par three seventh at Boulder Creek in Streetsboro, Ohio, places a premium on distance control. Back-tee shots need to carry at least 160 yards but not more than 175, while the uppermost tee is 117 yards from the green. Short or long tee shots put par at serious risk.

HOLE 8: The eighth hole at the Gary Player River Falls Plantation in Duncan, South Carolina, is one of the tougher par fours I've played. The longer you strive to hit your tee shot, the narrower the landing zone. A fade is best. This is one hole where "the dreaded straight ball" might very well be lost forever. The second shot is no box of chocolates either. I don't grumble if I walk off with a bogey.

HOLE 9: At my home club, Glen Eagle in Naples, Florida, we love our par five ninth hole. Top golfers regularly putt for eagle on 9, but most of us common golfers are content with knocking it on in three to set up for a birdie putt. We're careful to steer clear of the right side's out-of-bounds and the pond that runs two hundred yards along the left side of the fairway.

The front nine often is the easier side, and that is indeed the case with my fantasy golf course. My favorite holes 10 through 18 feature enough undulating greens and penalty areas to challenge any golfer, regardless of skills and experience. So refill your water bottle and let's go play the tough-as-nails backside.

HOLE 10: If Satan had a golf course, the tenth at Flying B in Salem, Ohio, would be the signature hole. A dogleg left, the hole is drivable length, but I know nobody who tries it. The green is guarded on the right by a steep-banked lake, and the left side plummets twenty feet to the cart path. Only precise pitch shots grab the tiny green. Even smart play can produce bad outcomes. Bogeys outnumber pars there, qualifying Flying B's tenth as the hole I love to hate.

Hole 10 at Flying B is dastardly difficult

HOLE 11: Once again, we're at Glen Eagle in Naples. Eleven is the hardest easy hole I've ever played. OB right, lake left and turning back toward the green to claim tee shots that might run through the fairway. Then you must deal with a three-tier green. I'll tell you how tough 11 is: I once lost the hole to my match-play opponent's 8. Ugh.

HOLE 12: I hope someday I will visit Switzerland, but until I do, I will always enjoy my own alpine vista from the tee box of Number 12 at Beaver Creek Meadows. Carved from the west wall of a river valley, the par three stretches more than two hundred yards from the lofty tee box to the oversized green rimmed front and right by a trickling stream. The size of the green belies the distance, as the golfer's eye can see the flag as closer than it actually is. The green may qualify as the most treacherous I've played. I once won the pin proximity prize on 12 but walked off with a 6.

HOLE 13: Think triskaidekaphobia on this one, Nicknamed Wee Bit of Hell, the short par four thirteenth at Links O'Tryon, Campobello, South Carolina, is bad luck for golfers who pitch short to the narrow green. Short is wet and long is perilous too, because chips back to the flag run down grain back to the pond. Take your par with a sigh of relief.

HOLE 14: In the tiny town of Edinburg, Pennsylvania, sprawled an interesting course named after the native Americans who once roamed there. Mohawk Trails is gone now, but its downhill dogleg-left par four fourteenth was one of the more dastardly holes ever created. I played there weekly for ten years and can remember only a few times when I got my second shot to stop on the green.

HOLE 15: We're back in Ohio for the last three holes. My favorite fifteenth is the infamous Z hole par five at Riverview near Warren, Ohio. The Z hole is a double dogleg left then right, with the right side bordered by the twisting Mahoning River. Only the bravest and most skilled players ever succeeded in getting on in two, and for most of us, even the third shot had to be hit purely to avoid plunking into the river. The massive green screamed three putt to me almost every time I played there.

HOLE 16: One of the nastiest par fives in my experience is the sixteenth at Kennsington in Canfield, Ohio. A long and straight tee shot is necessary for anyone trying for the green in two. The second shot can be a layup, but even then, the shot to the green must carry a brushy ravine, bunkers, and a mound. The green is huge and tricky. Birdies come often, but so do the double bogeys.

HOLE 17: I love the par three seventeenth at Pleasantview, near Paris, Ohio. It's a pretty spot, with a glistening lake stretching from tee box to the green and a hill behind the green to serve up perspective to the hopeful golfer. I love it too because it was the site of my recent hole in one, though I admit I exclaimed, "Oh, $#%&!" on impact, only to watch the ball plop, roll, and drop out of sight. That's golf!

HOLE 18: Every golfer knows the finishing hole must make a statement. I've played more than 110 golf courses, many of them hundreds of times each, so I speak from authority when I declare the best closing statement in my experience is the uphill par four at Reserve Run in Boardman,

Ohio. The tee shot is to a narrow fairway. The second shot must climb rapidly to the elevated, long, and narrow green, where the putting is complicated by confusing breaks that seemingly defy gravity. A par on RR's eighteenth sends us to the bar with grins.

The uphill Hole 18 at Reserve Run is the author's favorite finishing hole.

So that's my fav eighteen. Selecting my favorites was an interesting exercise. It wasn't easy to make my choices. But I'm glad I tried.

Here, as promised, is the all-inclusive list of golf courses I have played:

OHIO: Mill Creek North, Mill Creek South, Copeland Hills, Valley, Flying B, Salem Hills, Salem Golf Club, Duck Creek, Riverview, Manakiki, Windmill Lakes, Brookside, Glenmoor, Youngstown CC, Squaw Creek, Trumbull CC, Avalon Lakes, Old Avalon, Candywood, Yankee Run, Bedford Trails, Lakeside, Old Dutch Mill, Pine Lakes, Doughton, Carroll Meadows, Beaver Creek Meadows, Boulder Creek, Deer Creek, Edgewater, Eagle Sticks, Oakwood, Aurora CC, Mahoning CC, Walnut Run, Lake Club, Tippecanoe CC, Reserve Run, Firestone Farms, Kennsington, River Greens, Great Trails, Pleasantview,

Tannenhauf, Sleepy Hollow, Buck Run, Ashland CC, Whispering Pines, Countryside, Knoll Run, The Quarry, Tamer Win, and Worthington Hills CC.

PENNSYLVANIA: Blackhawk, Rolling Hills, Rolling Acres, Fox Run, Tanglewood, Castle Hills, Tam-O-Shanter, Oak Tree, Mohawk Trails, Ponderosa, Hunter's Station, Olde Stonewall, and North Hills CC.

FLORIDA: Glen Eagle, Tiburon, Naples Heritage, Naples Grande, Naples Lakes, Cedar Hammock, The Glades, Shadowood, Hibiscus, Foxfire, Old Corkscrew, Valencia, The National Ave Maria, Colliers Reserve, Windstar, and PGA National.

SOUTH CAROLINA: River Falls Plantation, Village Greens, Furman, Woodfin Ridge, Willow Creek, Links O'Tryon, River Hills, Myrtle Beach National, Eagle Nest, and Waterway Hills.

NORTH CAROLINA: Pinehurst 1, Pinehurst 3, Pinehurst 5, Pinehurst 6, Seven Lakes, Longleaf, Foxfire, Legacy, Seascape, Nags Head Links, Pointview, Carolina Club, and Goose Creek.

ALABAMA: Oxmoor Ridge, Craft Farms, Gulf Shores, and Lost Key.

CALIFORNIA: Pebble Beach and Spyglass.

MASSACHUSETTS: Falmouth CC and Dennis Pines.

NEW YORK: Maplehurst.

WEST VIRGINIA: Williams CC.

So what is your favorite eighteen? Get a sheet of paper and a pen. Before you move on to the next chapter, take a few moments to jot down your favorite eighteen holes and, when you are satisfied with your list, post it on your social media feed. Have some fun with it because it is, after all, your fantasy.

CHAPTER 27

Whiskey, beer, and golf

The celebration of the round may include a glass of Scotch or bourbon, certainly a beer or two, but not so much a cosmo or cabernet, though they are perfectly acceptable.

Something about golf seems to link it easily with alcoholic beverages. Yes, other sports are often enjoyed while sipping a comforting drink. A day at the ballpark seems to be better with a beer and a hot dog. It's as natural a sporting custom as I can imagine.

But golf has been associated with a few pops for just about as long as the game has been played. A popular belief is that a bottle of Scotch is good for eighteen shots, so ancient players were finished with their rounds when their bottles ran dry, thus leading to the development of eighteen-hole golf courses. That's what they say at the Old Course in St. Andrews.

(Parenthetically speaking, you can impress your friends by keeping them spellbound in explaining that American and Irish golfers drink whiskey, while Canadians, Brits, and Scots drink whisky. And you wouldn't order a whiskey in Scotland when you actually wanted a pour of whisky. Got that?)

In golf, the tradition of celebrating the day's game is here to stay.

But golf also is a sporting activity that tolerates—and even encourages—drinking while playing. You might find a cooler filled with beer and ice near the bench at a softball game, but most players don't take their drink to the batter's box.

Golf (and bowling, to name one other sport) does not frown on downing a drink in the midst of the action. It is so accepted, in fact, that many golf courses send out "beer girls" to make sure no golfers are playing thirsty. Interestingly, courses don't typically hire men for the job of operating a beverage cart. I think I know why, but I'll leave it up to you to figure it out.

The laws in most states forbid golfers from bringing their own booze to the course if it happens to have a liquor sale permit. Drinking is not prohibited as long as you purchase the alcohol from the golf course. Don't blame the course management. It's the law.

Properly permitted courses will set you up for buzzed fun right in the pro shop or on-site bar. The staff will sell cans of beer and even provide coolers and ice. At many courses, golfers also can stock up on airline-size "nips" of stronger stuff.

For most of my golfing life, I lived with the innocent belief that the celebration of birdies happened only at the end of the round, back at the

Golfers celebrate birdies with a nip of birdie juice.

clubhouse where we retreated to the bar to settle our wagers and reward ourselves with beers. I had no clue of the pervasiveness of a culture that adheres to a ritual of celebrating birdies immediately when they happen—often greenside, but rarely no later than your arrival at the next tee.

I also had no clue that a term exists for the celebration. It is "birdie juice." Well, that really does sum it up, yes?

Birdie juice is pretty much whatever you want it to be. I was intrigued to discover that birdie juice is not restricted to male golfers—though the chosen liquor often does tend to go along gender lines. Some birdie juice practitioners pack flasks in their golf bags. Others pack single-serving bottles of booze. Ladies typically go for smoother blends, perhaps Kahlúa, schnapps, or premixed cocktails like piña coladas, Long Island iced teas, or margaritas. Men will reach for whiskey, vodka, or Scotch, but really anything goes. Fireball is popular with the girls and the guys.

The call to celebrate is "Who wants birdie juice?" It's just a sip, so most golfers don't pass up the party. Four plastic shot glasses appear, short pours are added, the customary toast is delivered, and then it's bottoms up.

Soon after I discovered the world of birdie juice, wife Barb sent me to the ABC store to buy a bottle of butterscotch schnapps and a small flask. I know, butterscotch wouldn't be my first booze flavor choice, but who am I to judge?

I found the stuff, handed it to the cashier to scan, and learned at that moment that the term was familiar far beyond our local club's gates. "So, birdie juice is all you need today?" Ah, yes.

Most of the golfers I know don't make enough birdies to get tipsy, but this is not to say I haven't seen my fair share of inebriated players. Drinking happens even when there is nothing in particular to celebrate. During a recent Bloody Mary tournament, a player in our foursome asked whether any of the rest of us saw two flags on the green. Someone in Barb's foursome a few years back was convinced a clubhead cover on the fairway was a wild animal, her insistence so comical that the other three ladies couldn't stop laughing.

Common sense would tell us the best golf is done by sober players. But we all know exceptions. Many years ago, the frequent winner in our

Sunday morning shootouts was a guy who would put away a six-pack of Amstel Lights on the front nine, then restock for the back side. He might have slurred his words, but he could hit the ball straight every time.

To drink or not is a personal choice. I am a proponent of neither drinking nor abstaining. But I do try to understand why alcohol and golf became intertwined, so I did a bit of googling. I learned the reasons then are similar to the reasons now. Golf is social. Alcohol can enhance the experience and relieve stress. A drink or two heightens celebrations and strengthens bonds. Bars were never far from the last hole.

So to answer my own question—why did ancient golfers drink?—the answer is clear to me. Because they could.

Meanwhile, anybody want a nip of butterscotch schnapps? I think it's going to be in the cabinet for a long time.

CHAPTER 28

Be careful out there

The scene was as eerie as anything I've ever seen on a golf course.

The golf cart was clearly visible in the water just off the cart path, clear evidence the rumor spreading around the club was true. A member had splashed down after veering off course. Her descent from the path to the pond was steep and bumpy over rocks arranged to make the pond pretty when the water was low. The angle of entry and steepness of the descent left many to wonder how she'd managed to avoid serious injury. By most estimations, her cart could easily have flipped and rolled.

There it sat, roof deep in the clear water, like a submarine resting on the ocean bottom. While some found humor in the accident—as you might expect—it did serve as a stark reminder that a golfer might actually find peril out there.

Cruel as it might be, all manner of trouble awaits golfers who either are in the wrong place at the wrong time or who let their guard down for a moment. With thousands of golf courses around the world in outdoors locales as diverse as beaches and deserts to hills and dales to forests and mountains, it's no wonder people might stumble into trouble.

Another recent cart incident, at the same golf course where the woman drove into the lake, resulted in a woman suffering a broken leg. That same course has been the scene of more broken bones, sprained knees and ankles, snake bites, and bug stings, along with innumerable trips, stumbles, fainting spells, and other accidents, some of them requiring the attention of first responders and ambulance rides for emergency treatment.

All that on just one course.

Put golfers of all ages and health conditions in rugged outdoor settings with rock hard objects flying 100 miles per hour propelled by sticks and clubs delivering the force of a sledgehammer wielded by a muscle man and riding in gasoline- and electric-powered two-seat carts capable of traveling 15 miles per hour and you have a potent formula for pending disaster.

The Pit of Despair is a reminder that misfortune lurks on every golf course.

Cart crashes, ball strikes, and flying shrapnel from broken clubs can cause a lot of harm. So can stepping in an animal hole or sunken drain; tripping over a curb, golf club, or tee marker; and slipping on pine straw, muddy slope, or simple wet grass.

Anything can happen any time we golf. A man died at one of my favorite golf courses when a tree, without warning, crashed down across the cart he was riding. Another man died from a bee sting at a course I play often. He drank in the bee while sipping a beer.

Canadian friend Ted Daugherty survived a harrowing attack from an agitated redtail hawk. The raptor apparently was defending her nest high in the tree near Ted when she swooped down toward his head and latched onto his scalp with needle sharp talons.

Boston buddy Jimmy Duggan wins my prize for the creepiest accident. He was set up for a shot under an overhanging branch when a snake dropped onto his shoulders. He said it was a pygmy rattlesnake. I'll take his word for it.

Another friend took a knockout shot in the forehead from a golf ball hooked from the adjacent fairway. That can happen at lots of places. That's why they call those tracks "hardhat courses."

I have been hit in the mouth with a golf ball and endured six stitches to fix my exploded lip. I've twisted ankles and wrenched my knee. I have overstretched my shoulders and worried about a damaged rotator cuff. I've suffered too many sunburns, liquid nitrogen blasts to destroy sun-sparked actinic keratoses, and the Mohs surgeon's knife to excise basal cell and squamous cell carcinomas.

None of that is a day at the beach.

But let me tell you this. If a screeching hawk clutches my forehead or I find myself wearing a three-foot snake necklace, I'm done for the day. I'm going to the bar, and nobody will stop me.

Good grief. It's golf, for crying out loud. Nobody told me it would hurt.

So, to quote Sergeant Phil Esterhaus of the old NBC TV show *Hill Street Blues*, "Let's be careful out there."

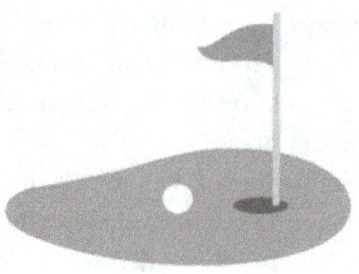

CHAPTER 29

Sunrise on the first tee

I have teed off during fourteen of the day's twenty-four hours, so I have had many opportunities to play the game in all manner of bright and dim conditions. Any time can be delightful, but the hour after sunrise is my favorite by far.

The moments after the sun peeks over the trees to our east are always amazing. Pastels no brush can paint streak the horizon. The day is fresh, the air is cool, and the coffee perks me to just the right mood. Best of all for the golfer, the scorecard is a blank canvas, ready to reflect the masterpiece about to be played.

Sunrise on the first tee is never to be taken for granted. I go ready for anything. For me, it is akin to sunrise on the water. When I go to the lake, I take only rods, reels, lures, and my instincts. Likewise, I go to sunrise tee times with nothing but the essentials for the next four hours of my day. Those and maybe a jug of water.

I have started rounds during all of the hours between 7:00 a.m. and 9:00 p.m. I have played in drizzle and driving rain, snow flurries and blizzards, blistering heat, numbing cold, gusting wind, and swirling leaves, under bright sky and in pitch darkness. I can recall golf highs and lows in all manner of conditions, but the ones that stand out forever are the ones that happened when the day was young and the card was still bogey free.

Poets and philosophers look deep into our souls and tell us of the goodness and inspiration that stir when the new day dawns, whether romanticized to the rhythm of iambic pentameter or couched in the context of the human condition. English philosopher Bernard Williams said, "There was never a night or a problem that could defeat sunrise or hope."

Well, then, doesn't that sum it up neatly? Sunrise brings hope and new beginnings regardless of whether you are a carpenter, schoolteacher, bass angler, or golfer.

At the first tee, I am rested, energized, and motivated. Distractions that might flow into my brain are few enough to be insignificant. When I get in my car for sunrise tee times, the news has not made headlines, the stock market is still sleeping, and rush-hour commuters are brushing their teeth.

Morning on the golf course is like a *Snow White* scene with dewy grounds and sleepy golfers. The sky is spectacular. Mist hangs over the low spots. The aroma of freshly mowed grass wafts to your nostrils along

At sunrise, the air is fresh, and the scorecard is a blank canvas.

with a hint of the mowers' gasoline-fired internal combustion smoke. Roosters crow, crows caw, and songbirds sing as the day gets going.

Sunrise tee times are especially wonderful in July and August when the morning news meteorologist is jabbering about a cloudless sky, torrid temperatures, and withering humidity. She's not worrying me when I know I'll be sitting in the shade, sipping a cold beer, and counting my winnings by the time the mercury tops ninety.

Neither does the wind play large when the sun is still low in the sky. No gusts to knock good shots to trouble. All is calm. Stillness is peace. Peace inspires joy. The golf course is that day's heaven.

From the clubhouse door, we scan the grounds as they slowly wipe the mist away. I spy the golf course hound, bounding across the first fairway, the tags on her collar jangling to the beat of her leaps and dashes.

It's as though she was sent to remind us that joy is there to be had if we open our hearts and leave our worries in the parking lot.

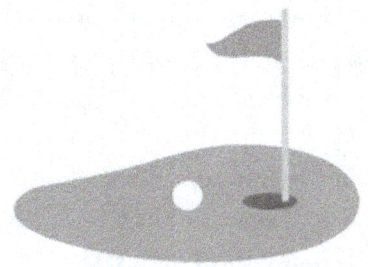

CHAPTER 30

It's a family affair

Wife Barb observed recently that golf is a sport in which a family foursome spanning four generations can play on even terms.

"Old-timers can't run, and little kids can't sit," she said as she watched three generations of golfers play past our vantage point. "Golf is the perfect outdoor family activity when you're mixing grandparents with grandchildren."

Families of golfers play regularly at our club in Naples, Florida, just as they do at thousands of golf courses across the nation and around the world.

As a high school girls golf coach for twenty years, Barb saw firsthand the investment of two and three generations of encouragement to youthful players. Grandparents and parents supported their girls in the interscholastic golf matches as Barb helped guide new generations of players into the game.

What's more, Barb is the middle member of a four-generation golf family—her grandfather, her mother and father, Barb herself, and our daughter Betsy, who began golfing with Mom, Dad, Pop, and Grandma at courses in Ohio and Florida around age nine.

Golf is a good game for elders to pass along their knowledge and passion as well as to teach rules, strategy, and technique. Yes, grandparents can play basketball and football with their grandchildren, but golf is a lot easier on the bodies of young and old. Like Barb says, "Old-timers can't run."

One of Coach Barb's recruiting statements for teen girls contemplating joining their high school golf team was the fact that golf is a game they could play for life. "You aren't going to play business soccer in your career, but you certainly will be able to play business golf," she counseled her young players.

Family golf is a way of life in many US communities. Country clubs' rosters often include multiple generations of families, and public courses' tee times are loaded with family foursomes.

It's all fun and games as adults introduce their kids to golf. Toddlers wielding big orange plastic clubs are common sights at picnics, parks, and backyard family time. Laughter and cheers erupt depending on the outcome of Junior's and Missy's best (and worst) swings. Who hasn't laughed at a video of a toddler swinging and whiffing?

This is not to say it is always easy to bring a young person along in the game of golf. I recall some pretty intense parent-child exchanges as we worked with our daughter to help her learn the game. Navigating the teen years is hard enough without trying to master short-game finesse, putting touch, and full-swing power and accuracy.

The PGA recognizes the potential. PGA Family Golf offers opportunities for parents and grandparents, brothers and sisters, aunts and uncles to form teams and play competitive golf. The PGA says the program is designed to bring families together through golf, noting on its website, "In sports, your team is your family. With PGA Family Golf, your family is your team."

That's cool. In this era when many people lament that young people don't get outdoors enough, that they spend too much time in their digital worlds, golf can be a motivator for young players. PGA Family Golf says healthy quality time by families outdoors is priceless.

Barb's family golf time dates back to the days she spent chipping in her parents' backyard. She and her father lobbed shots at target trees and laughed at the good shots and bad. She learned well, and her father encouraged her, at age twelve, to enter a pitch-and-putt tournament at The Cloister resort at Sea Island, Georgia. She won the first-place trophy.

Her family link to the game coursed through her veins. Her maternal grandfather emigrated to the US from Scotland and enjoyed many rounds of business golf as a member at Youngstown Country Club during that city's heyday in steelmaking and other heavy industry. Young

Barbie picked up on the country club vibe during many giggling golf cart rides with her grandfather around the grand old course.

Our family connection to golf remains strong, as a fourth generation is getting active in the game. Daughter Betsy Wollitz Khan and her husband, Dr. Irfan Khan, have joined Worthington Hills Country Club in Columbus, Ohio. I'm sure great-grandpa Jack Carson and grandparents Don and Betty Woods are smiling down in approval.

Proud parents Barb and Jack give thumbs-up too of course, with Barb and Betsy already strategizing to move up from their second-place finish in the 2025 Glen Eagle Ladies Member-Guest. Irfan and I plan to shave a few strokes from our total in The Talon member-guest in 2026.

Fun and games. That's what it's all about. Done right, lifetimes of enjoyment are the dividends of time wisely invested in family rounds of golf.

Pebble Beach was a bucket-list round for the author; his wife, Barb; daughter Betsy Wollitz Khan; and son-in-law Irfan Khan.

CHAPTER 31

Beating the darkness

One golf hazard always wins. Darkness. It is the relentless foe, the impenetrable thicket, the deepest water, and the grossest gorse.

Golfing through twilight is one of the many unique experiences associated with life on the links. It's not just the setting sun that sets the tone; it is a combination of circumstances that defines the game for millions of golfers.

Teeing off when the sun is low in the west is a bonus for some and a necessity for many. It is a bonus for those who prefer to beat the heat or add an extra nine holes to a busy day. It is a necessity for the working person whose eight-to-five job precludes midday outings on the course.

But to win twilight golf, one must putt out before darkness envelopes the course. It is you against the sun, a race well worth running.

I was among those who squeezed in weeknight rounds during spring and summer. They were my only opportunities for weekday golf because of the hours I spent on the job. I was very grateful to golf those Monday evenings between May and September. I used to quip that the after-work golf league I joined in the early 1990s was the only good thing about Mondays.

Whether it is a bonus or necessity, evening golf is different. The light is different. The temperature and humidity are different. The feeling is different. The sounds are different. The course itself is different for the evening golfer.

Hitting into the setting sun adds another degree of difficulty. The coolness and humidity can affect the ball flight. The general atmosphere is serene, as bird songs' volume rises and traffic sounds decline. The grass grows longer, and the greens get slower.

The blues are bluer, the greens are greener, and the red-and-orange sunsets are sharper than the brand-new Crayolas in the sixty-four-packs the kids took to school.

My first-ever eagle happened one evening as the sun dipped to the tree line.

Barb and I grabbed a burger after work and ate in the car as we drove to our local muni, a course she knew like the back of her hand. It was the home track for her Boardman High School girls' golf team, where she'd played varsity a decade before our twilight round.

Always one quick with a quip, she dubbed the first nine on Mill Creek's North Course the "fainting nine" because one of her teammates went down for the count on a steamy afternoon. Her friend Rosie survived of course, but the hole on which she hit the turf, Number 4, is forever the "fainting hole" in Barb's mind.

I teed up and struck an average drive down the left side of the fairway of Number 4. As we walked to our second shots, Barb recalled the story of Rosie feeling woozy and crumpling to the grass. We found our balls, mine resting nicely on the fairway 155 yards from the hole, and waited for the twosome in front of us to putt out. The sun was dropping like a rock toward the western horizon.

The glare made it difficult to distinguish forms on the green, but I judged that by the time I would be ready to swing, the two men would be on their way to the fifth tee box. I lined up my iron shot, made the swing, and felt the pure pleasure of a perfect impact.

"Why did you hit?" Barb said as the ball rocketed toward the green. "Those guys are still on the green!"

Oops. I'd misjudged the pace of the pair up ahead and pulled the trigger a moment too soon.

"Fore!"

The ball landed on the front of the green, safely away from the turtle walkers, and rolled toward the hole, then disappeared. The men raised their arms, not in protest, but in celebration of my fortunate shot.

Thank goodness it didn't hit them. We would have had to rename Number 4 the KO hole. It was nevertheless my first-ever eagle and a shot

I will never forget.

Twilight golf kick-started my workweek for more than thirty years. I joined a Monday evening golf league at a course near home in Youngstown, Ohio, and snuck out of the office (don't tell the boss) an hour early to make it to the course in time for league play. The fact I always worked an hour or so from home complicated my efforts to get to the course with enough daylight for nine holes. But I always made it, and I actually credit my creativity in getting to the first tee before the last foursome departed. The truth is, of course, the first drive of the evening can be tough enough without dealing with elevated blood pressure caused by the race to get to the course.

I loved those Monday evening rounds. The league roster included dozens of great guys, some good golfers and some not so good, but we all had fun and laughed about bonehead shots, celebrated birdies, and cried over missed putts. By eight o'clock each Monday evening, the worries at home and the troubles at work were shoved to the side, and only the game and the guys mattered.

Twilight melted to darkness on more than a few evenings. As the member with the longest commute to the course, I often was in the last foursome, where vision mattered little when it came to locating the rounds' final shots. "Anybody see where it went?" was a common question. "I think I heard it hit a tree" was a common answer.

Darkness sometimes beat us to the last hole, but nobody could call themselves losers after finishing with the knowledge that cold beer and good buddies were waiting for us to join them.

We beat the darkness and had another headful of stories to take to regale the crowd at the bar.

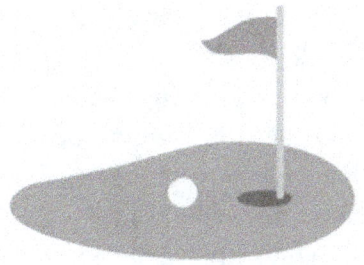

CHAPTER 32

Things that go bump in the night

It was a long time ago, so I do not recall whether the starter signaled with a rocket or shotgun, but the first shot of my first night golf tournament was a blast.

Within a few moments of the go signal, orbs of light arced across the fairways. It was a sight to behold.

The event was a four-person scramble over six of the holes on the front nine at the club where wife Barb's parents played. Three of the holes were bypassed for safety's sake, as water loomed large enough to pose the potential for drowning golf carts. Good move.

In the pitch darkness, the players used hard plastic balls into which we inserted glow sticks. They proved to be relatively easy to see, if only while resting at our feet as we prepared to swing. Finding them on the golf course was not quite as easy.

Nevertheless, we played on. We aimed at flagsticks to which glow sticks were strapped. Yardage was anybody's guess, so the best guessers set us up for birdie putts on several holes.

I do not recall our final score, but I do know we won the event. And so concluded my first after-dark golf experience.

Needless to say, golfing in the dark is quite different from the daytime game. Vision is limited, of course, and one's depth perception is skewed. Reading the greens is a guessing game, and figuring out where the next hole is located is challenging.

Night golf ups the odds for a pure whiff. Fat and thin shots outnumber the pure strikes. If your round takes longer than a couple of hours, you run the risk of your ball's glow stick losing its light.

Golf is hard enough without playing the game in the dark, and yet I opted to play in several other night tournaments in subsequent years. The night game is difficult yet intriguing, so I said yes when friends invited us to play in their club's night event.

The day of the tournament, a full-on head cold bloomed in my sinuses and chest. I'd been looking forward to the fun, especially since it was the Halloween season and witches and ghosts would be prowling the grounds. I popped an antihistamine as we arrived at the course—as the temperature dropped to less than 40 degrees—and loaded our clubs on the waiting golf cart.

The parking lot was dark, but we somehow managed to avoid running over any other golfers, then checked in with our friends and the tournament director. Barb asked the question that was on her mind earlier as we drove to the golf course.

"What's the prize for winning?"

"Prize? There are no prizes. But we have pizza and cookies for when you finish."

I recall we both wondered WTF?

Anyway, off we went, me coughing, sneezing, and blowing my nose. My team couldn't see me in the dark, but they certainly could hear me. Nine holes came and went, and the glowing orbs lit up the fairways like an earthly meteor shower. Out in the dark we heard cheers and groans—the same sounds, interestingly enough, one would hear in the daytime.

Our round concluded, we packed our clubs in the trunk of the car and headed to the clubhouse for pizza and cookies. Turns out there was a little prize money after all, which we learned when the director brought a dollar to our table and announced we'd won a skin.

Our host paid us each a quarter. Two bits for all that fun. Plus we got to keep the glow necklaces we received at registration. Cheap thrills, all things considered, as we survived the things that went bump in the night.

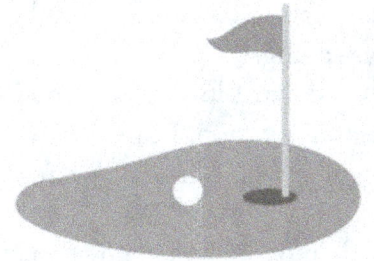

CHAPTER 33
Lost and found

I could tell by the tone in his voice that my friend was in distress.

"Jack," he implored, "did you pick up a silver dollar?"

Cosmo Pecchia has been a golf buddy for thirty years. He's also my barber, a profession he'd begun thirty years before I met him. During his more than sixty years circling his chair and scissoring clients' hair, Cosmo has met a cast of characters longer than a 7,400-yard championship golf course.

One of them was a kind old customer who handed Cosmo a silver dollar, a gesture for which the old-timer was well-known. For more than ten years, Cosmo had carried the silver coin in his pocket while golfing, a good-luck charm to ward off bogeys and other bad fortune. It has worked for him, as Cosmo, now in his mideighties, can still shoot his age. He's also had a pair of aces in recent years.

As fate would have it, Cosmo rode with me to the golf course that day. Back in the car for the ride home, he fretted about the lost keepsake. He had already frisked his pockets, inspected his golf bag several times, and searched the car's floor mats and seat cushions.

"I know I had it with me this morning. I can't imagine I left it out there."

He was heartbroken, but soon resolved that the silver dollar was gone.

Then my phone buzzed this morning. The caller ID showed "Cosmo Barber Shop."

"Hello, Cosmo!"

"Jack, how the heck are you? You'll never guess why I'm calling." At that moment, we were 1,250 miles from each other's location, so yes, I had no idea why he was calling.

"Remember that silver dollar I lost last summer? I found it! It was on the floor in the restroom at my shop! I can't believe it. It's a miracle!"

Good for Cosmo, a golfer who can again tee it up with Lady Luck on his side.

Lost items are more than dashed luck, however, as I have experienced personally and witnessed with friends. Two commonly lost items are putter covers and wedges. Putter covers can be shrugged aside. They have little sentimental value, and I don't know anybody who puts faith in the magic of their putter covers. For twenty-five dollars, they can easily be replaced.

I recently lost a wedge, which is a bit more traumatic. They cost a lot of money, for one thing, but they also can have sentimental value, either as a treasured hand-me-down or as the club that carried a golfer to a memorable score. After I realized my sand wedge was missing, I played three holes with a heavy heart and bogey scores. Then I decided to drive back to the trailing foursome and discovered a friend had picked up my wedge and was going to take it to lost and found at the turn. Never mind my name and address were on a label on the shaft. My mood improved considerably after retrieving the club.

Even a keepsake ball marker or a favorite hat can ruin the day when it turns up missing. Angst over lost items is a compound problem in fact, as the loser often is distracted by retracing steps and creating a search strategy, and fretting over the void left by their disappearances.

The older I get, the lost-stuff experiences continue to pile up. Who hasn't left a wind shirt in the golf cart basket, a water bottle in the cup holder, or their cell phone in the cubby? Nine times out of ten, the item is returned or discovered in the club's lost-and-found box. No harm, no foul, right?

I did feel harmed, however, over the disappearance of my range finder. I treasured the device, a Father's Day gift, which quickly became my indispensable caddie. I was shattered, therefore, when I could not locate the range finder as I unloaded my stuff at home after a day at the course. I immediately called the golf shop to alert them about my lost item, and the attendant said he would check the lost-and-found. I called back an hour later and learned nobody had turned in my range finder, but the pro shop guy assured me the club's players were an honest lot, so he was confident my item would be located in a day or two.

I brooded the balance of the day and on into the next. I'd owned the gadget for just a few weeks, but it already had gained sentimental value. It was just a "thing," for sure, but I felt a hole in my soul—and certainly in my ability to accurately determine the distance between me and the hole.

Luck was on Cosmo Pecchia's side on this November day in Ohio when he scored a hole-in-one

I called the golf course again. Nope. No range finder matching the description of mine had been turned in. I got the same story the next day.

So I reckon the "finders keepers" motto directed the conscience of whoever found my range finder. Perhaps the term "finders keepers" is too benevolent. The finder could not have known how much I valued my range finder or how quickly it had gained importance to me, but even if they had, would they have fought off their larcenous inclination?

We'll never know. But the experience is a reminder about the self-policing ethics of the game. If it feels wrong, don't do it. If you think nobody is looking, think again. If you think nobody is counting, don't believe it. If you find somebody's stuff, return it.

Remember, lost and found is a good thing. Finders keepers, not so much.

One last thought: It's a good thing we don't get too attached to our golf balls. You know what I mean, right?

CHAPTER 34
A little rain will fall

As I begin this chapter, I am investing time made available because I canceled my 7:48 a.m. tee time. Begging out seemed prudent since the temperature was 47 degrees and the 20 mph north wind was driving rain sideways. Though I admit I hesitated before picking up my phone to call the pro shop, I succumbed to the conditions and canceled.

Frank at the pro shop agreed I made a good choice, as did dozens of others that morning who wisely calculated that with 75 degree weather returning in a day or two, canceling our morning round was prudent.

It's not like my play that day was at Royal Troon. It was in Naples, Florida, where the sun shines virtually every day and the temperature ranges from comfy warm to swelteringly hot throughout the year. While "winter" in Naples is a relative matter compared to the winters of most of the world's golfers, Southwest Florida residents and snowbirds are known sometimes to "suffer" through rainy 47-degree sunrises.

Golf is rarely out of the question in SW Florida. If you can't golf today, just go tomorrow instead.

This morning's decision made, I poured another cup of coffee and began to ponder a serious question: Why did I even hesitate to cancel?

Rain is a given in much of the golfing world, but golfers own polar-opposite views about playing under precipitation. "Never!" say many. "Grab your umbrella and let's go!" say others.

The sport was born in rainy climes. Dreary days under scuds of lead-colored clouds were expected in Scotland. Today's U.K. golf travel advisers recommend visiting players pack rain suits because it is so likely they will experience foul weather.

A morning like today's would probably be a different situation if my tee time was in Scotland. I'd pack my rain suit and head over to the first tee.

I suppose my hesitation to cancel this morning was borne of two factors: my appreciation for the legacy of golf and my own optimism that good weather could arrive at any moment.

We are taught to accept in life that "a little rain will fall" to cope with the times when things aren't going well. In golf, yes, a little rain will fall, but is it always a bad thing, especially if we have any of the DNA of our golfer ancestors?

Here's what I think, though I fully understand that many people – including my Florida friends – will disagree, some mildly and some wholeheartedly. I think golf, like football, is meant to be played in reasonable rain.

Rain never stops a football game, but it's a no-no in baseball and tennis, where slippery, squishy balls can become dangerous. Rain is fine in Formula One auto racing, but brings out the red flag in American oval-track motorsports.

In golf, as I mentioned, the expectation is that play can continue under reasonable conditions. "Reasonable" is a personal matter. What's reasonable for you might be a miserable soaking for another.

In days long gone, I did not worry about rain. I once played (and survived) a fundraiser scramble, the entirety of its six hours contested under a steady, soaking and eventually bone-chilling rain. Hot food and cold beer at the end were our inspiration to forge forward.

When it rains is another factor. Some say it's OK to continue playing through rain that starts during the round, but they would never go to the first tee with a rain cloud overhead. Some will interrupt a round to sit at a shelter or back at the clubhouse to ride out a rainstorm, then return to the course when the clouds part.

A popular school of thinking among my Florida golf buddies is "why golf in the rain when we don't have to?" But among my Ohio friends, the prevailing attitude is "I don't think the hard stuff is supposed to come until we're finished."

All of this is to say we deal with rain in our own personal ways.

So, back to my question: Why did I hesitate to cancel this morning?

The answer is that the optimist in me held hope that the forecast was wrong, the clouds would part and blue sky would welcome me at the first tee. But I tempered my optimism with my real-world experience that despite believing I am going to shoot a great score, a little rain always falls on my parade to par. So the decision was easy, if not immediate:

"Hey, Frank, scratch me today."

CHAPTER 35

Snow, frozen ponds, frosty greens, and other favorites

You call yourself a golfer and yet you've never lofted a wedge shot to a rock-hard green and cringed as it bounded 50 feet into the air, not once, but three or four times? Have you ever been forced to invoke the two-putt rule because the greens had an inch or two of snow? Never lost a golf ball plugged in the last unmelted snowdrift? How many times have you chipped a ball off an ice-covered greenside pond?

While I won't go so far as to say every true golfer must strike a shot off a frozen pond before he or she can claim to have played in inclement weather, I will say winter golf is certainly a fifth dimension to the game we love to play. Mathematicians and physicists tell us a fifth dimension is hypothetical, but I'm here to tell you I've been there and returned to current space and time successfully.

"There" is the wonderful world of winter golf.

I chuckle today at Florida friends who shudder at the thought of teeing off in sub-60-degree weather. They'd rather be stripped naked, covered with honey and staked to an anthill than endure 18 holes in cold weather.

OK, to each his or her own.

Full disclosure here before I write on: I do prefer a sunny 80-degree day for my golf. The sun warms the bones, loosens the muscles, and removes shivering from the distractions. It's easy to relax and find focus when the conditions are so patently neutral.

So while I am not saying I'd select 30 degrees over 80 and snow over sunshine, I am also not going to say I haven't found special joy in completing 18 holes while most golfers are huddling under blankets in front of their fireplaces. The satisfaction of not only setting out on a wintery day, but also putting out on 18, extends far beyond the numbers on the scorecard. A deeper-than-typical sense of accomplishment settles into the winter golfer's soul on the drive home, where a hot meal, crackling fire and cozy recliner are the rewards for the effort you've invested in the game you enjoy.

Like most other rounds of golf, the winter game is best played with a band of buddies. Winter golf groups exist around the world, including in my corner of Ohio, where I survived the dreary months of December through February by looking beyond the Monday-to-Friday grind with the knowledge that Sunday morning would find me in the clubhouse of our winter track, selecting teams, putting up our money, and trash-talking about who might be that day's hero.

I prefer warm and sunny, but the game was born where nasty weather is common.

One winter season was not especially harsh. It might snow on Tuesday, melt by Thursday and remain dry through Sunday. That weather pattern carried from Christmas to St. Patrick's Day, at which point spring sprung and we were playing in shorts.

Other winters were less favorable. I recall one day when we teed off with the thermometer showing a balmy 15 degrees. Golf friend Cosmo split a Maxfli on his first tee shot, turned and nonchalantly asked, "Which half do I play?" We graciously granted him a mulligan.

At this point, you probably are wondering what kind of near-sighted golf course owner would let players tread across his precious greens under such nasty conditions. We learned, of course, that frosty greens could suffer damage inflicted by golfers walking across them. The boss did invoke the confounding "frost delay" when the turf was not frozen, but the blades of grass were frosty. After the ground froze, however, he had no problem turning golfers loose, explaining that frozen greens would not suffer foot-traffic damage. In fact, the course's greens were perfectly healthy come spring and summer.

So off we went, Sunday after Sunday, during the 20 years our group stayed intact.

The second hole was an all-carry par 3, protected in the front by a pond. The cart path cut diagonally between the water's edge and the green, so a punch-and-run shot was pretty much out of the question. We opted for high-loft clubs and tried to drop shots short of the pin, with high hopes they would somehow find a landing spot soft enough to absorb the ball's energy. It hardly ever worked. Most of the shots fell out of the sky like, well, speeding golf balls, rebounded off the frozen turf and rocketed up again nearly as high as the apex of the tee shot itself. We invariably were forced to play slippery down-hill chip shots that skipped and skidded like hockey pucks across rink ice.

Pars were like pennies from heaven. Birdies were so rare, that a deuce on number 2 was golden. Bogies were OK and doubles were not uncommon.

Such is winter golf – or, at least, the version that my gang played.

Hole four was our ego-booster. At 320 yards, the hole proved to be reachable for many in our Sunday group, not because of our length, but because frozen fairways are like airport runways. A 240-yard carry might end with 75 or 80 yards of roll. Cool, yes, but the same conditions turned short shots into guessing games. How much would they skid and run?

Truth is, the satisfaction of striking the perfect wedge often turned into a groan of despair when the ball bounced high three times before coming to rest 20 yards beyond the green.

Many times our group teed off under a sunny sky only to finish in a miniblizzard. Around hole 14 or 15, the greens might have accumulated an inch of wet snow, which clung to putts as they rolled toward the hole.

Those were the days when orange and chartreuse golf balls were put into play, simply because they were easier to find on flurry-littered fairways.

Were we cold? Not really. I recall some of our guys muttering about their sanity as we stomped around the first tee, but by the end of the day, nobody had frostbite. We dressed for the weather, walked, and carried or dragged our own bags. By the third hole, the temperature, whether 25 or 45, was not a factor, as the exercise burned calories and body heat prompted us to shed some of the bulky outer layers.

I thoroughly enjoyed those winters of golf and often reflect on the happy times. Of course, I was younger, and my body had not soaked up so many years of wear and tear, medicine and surgeries.

Nevertheless, I learned 30 degrees is just a number on a thermometer, a number that is irrelevant when extraordinary circumstances come calling.

Some of my Sunday golf buddies, too many, in fact, have passed on, but the warm memories of what we all achieved are like so many birdies on the scorecard of life. They are exquisite reminders of those days when we dug deep into ourselves and for four hours at a time experienced a fifth dimension of our existence.

CHAPTER 36

What hit me?

I should have seen it coming.

The sun was low in the western sky as my foursome putted out and walked off the eighteenth green. Our after-work Monday golf league was, in my opinion, a great way to get the week started. The workday flew faster with my knowing the reward awaiting after my eight hours in the office.

I was typically in the league's final foursome due to the fact my workplace was one hour's drive from the golf course. For that reason, I usually finished in twilight conditions.

So it is understandable that I didn't see it coming, and then, it did.

The impact spun my head and flung my glasses. My first thought was "What hit me?" My second thought was "Why are my three friends staring wide-eyed at my face?

Bill offered a clean white towel he pulled out of his bag. "Hold this to your mouth." I obeyed, pressing firmly on the sore spot on my upper lip. As guys do, I pulled the towel away to inspect what it had absorbed. I was shocked at the size of the crimson blot.

The foursome that had been waiting in the fairway for our exit off 18 jogged up to the green. Apologies flew fast and furious. The blood, meanwhile, soaked the cloth, no longer the clean white towel Bill had handed me moments earlier.

We walked to the pavilion, where the golf course permitted our league to keep a locked refrigerator stocked with longnecks and a gas grill for cooking hot dogs. Word reached the pavilion before our arrival, and we were greeted by curiosity seekers. Like motorists gawking at an auto accident scene, my golf buddies stared at my twisted lip, already swelling around the gaping wound. The bleeding slowed, and I fidgeted in my pocket for a dollar to buy a beer.

"Not tonight, Jack," counseled the league boss. "I think you should go to the ER."

Oh, wow. Was it that bad?

Yes, apparently it was. In fact, the ER doc stalled long enough after his initial cleanup to make me and wife Barb begin to suspect he didn't want to stitch the hole closed. She had met me at the hospital after I called to inform her I'd been hit in the mouth by an approach shot thinned by a golfer one hundred yards from the green.

"What do you think?" Barb asked the doctor.

"I think he should see a plastic surgeon," he replied.

Oh, wow. So the next morning, I called the office to say I was going to be late because—wait for it—I'd been hit by a golf ball. Yeah, sure.

Truth is a lot can go wrong out on the golf course. I'm not especially accident-prone, but I have had my share of mishaps. I've twisted an ankle, sprained my shoulder, suffered golfer's elbow, slashed my arm on saw-blade palmettos, and soaked up enough sunlight to breed hundreds of actinic keratosis inflammations necessitating twice-a-year body scans by my dermatologists.

Of course, not all of my ailments are golf related. I fish as often as I golf, so my lifestyle puts me in harm's way more frequently than the Average Jack. I've been snagged by treble hooks, tumbled overboard, and fallen victim to the overpowering nausea of seasickness. A hurtling jig, launched by a friend's eager hookset, busted my lip on the side opposite the golf ball wound, and an orthopedic surgeon repaired carpometacarpal damage to both hands caused by too many hundreds of thousands of casts.

So I should have seen it coming. If we put ourselves in harm's way too often, eventually harm will find us.

Be careful out there.

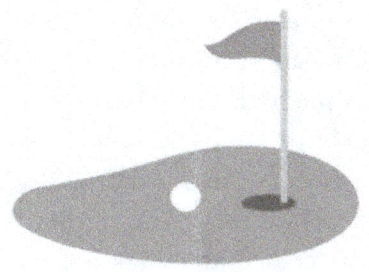

CHAPTER 37

Did that just happen?

Just when you think nothing will ever again shock you, along comes another bolt of lightning.

Wife Barb and I were enjoying a midweek evening nine holes with the promise of a fast-food burger stop after our round. Young daughter Betsy was tagging along. The temperature could not have been nicer, and the sky showed no sign of threatening weather. A chorus of crows cawed approval in the trees. All in all, it was one fine way to cap off another nice day in hometown Ohio.

The sound of a distant siren gained volume. An emergency vehicle was on the move, obviously heading our way. We feared not, however, as we were a quarter mile from the highway, so we turned our focus back to our second shots on the par four sixth hole.

Our concentration was distracted, however, as the volume was amplified by engine noise now accompanying the siren. A weird, muffled thumping joined the ruckus.

Then we saw it, a full-blown police car chase at full throttle across the golf course and now bearing down on us on the sixth fairway. Taking no chance as this cops-and-robbers scenario raced toward us in fading light, we ducked out of the way. The fleeing car and cruiser roared past us, ripped across the green, bounded over the ditch separating the golf course from a neighboring cornfield, and disappeared into the twilight like the sheriff pursuing the General Lee in a *Dukes of Hazzard* episode.

Barb and I, shaken, looked at each other in utter amazement. Did that just happen?

Chalk that one up to another weird experience at places where weirdness can take many shapes and sizes.

We've all experienced the odd shots that carom off trees and ricochet off rocks to end up safely in play. My best round ever included three shots that found the fairway despite trajectories that should have resulted in lost balls. I converted two of them into birdies.

I know a golfer whose tee ball literally knocked a bird out of the sky, killing the creature as surely as Randy Johnson KO'd that dove during spring training in Arizona.

Everybody has experienced some ill-timed sprinkler incidents, including one of the girls on the opposing team in a match with the Poland (Ohio) Seminary High School team Barb coached. She was getting ready to hit when the sprinkler head she was straddling popped up out of the fairway and shot a jet of water directly at her. The screams could be heard for miles.

Yes, that did happen.

So did the Great Walking Ball Marker incident during another of Barb's high school matches. A player on the opposing team opted to mark her ball with an insect she plucked from the putting surface. She believed the insect was dead and decided it was a perfectly legit marker. Before she could replace her ball, however, the marker came to life and walked away.

Talk about weird shots. I recall one my childhood friend Jack hit. It was like a trick shot on a pool table. Jack teed up, swung, and ticked the ball, which flicked toward the tee marker, striking it squarely and spinning back to the exact spot from which he had hit it.

Many years ago, at one of the NEC championships at Firestone Country Club, our young daughter, Betsy, carefully eyed the approaching golfers while sitting on her greenside stool. Sharp-eyed, she spied the rocketing wedge launched by Phil Mickelson. Suspecting she was in the landing zone, she stood and strolled a few paces away, just in time to avoid the arrival of the approach shot, which trampolined off the stool. Had she not moved, the ball would have hit her. Whatever prompted her to stand at that moment was purely fortuitous. It's a good thing she did, or we would have spent the balance of the day in the local ER.

While we can be in the wrong place at the wrong time, we also sometimes are in the right place at the right time.

During the 1994 Solheim Cup at The Greenbrier in White Sulphur Springs, West Virginia, Betsy was standing at the roped-off path the golfers used to pass from the green to the next tee. After European team golfer Annika Sörenstam holed her putt and walked to the exit lane, she smiled at and handed her ball to Betsy, who was thrilled to receive such a prized keepsake.

Did that just happen? Indeed it did, and twenty years later, Annika happily signed the ball at a reception Barb and I attended.

Weird events sometimes stir controversy.

On the first hole during a round many years ago, the friendly golf course dog was romping across the fairway, seemingly exhilarated by the fresh morning air and the multitude of golfers. We hit our tee shots and proceeded up the fairway when the dog, a muscular reddish boxer, scooped up one of our balls and bounded away to points unknown. The ensuing conversation covered all the imaginable arguments—from "play

You need to be ready for anything out there, even a bear romping across the first fairway at Glen Eagle in Naples, Florida.

it where she drops it" to "how many penalty strokes for that mischief?"

Of course, we did settle on simply replacing the ball at the point nearest where we last knew it to be. But yes, that did happen.

Late one day many, many summers ago, Barb and I survived another harrowing experience, ironically on the same golf course where the police chase occurred. We had made it blissfully carefree to the ninth tee as the sun dipped below the tree line to our west. I hit first, hoping for a safe landing in a fair lie. Barb walloped her drive, and off we walked into the twilight.

At first, they just buzzed our ears, but then we felt them brush against our cheeks and legs. Soon I was swatting and Barb was flailing as the world's largest swarm of mosquitoes decided to feast on our blood. Problem was we each had only one arm for defense, as the other was dragging our pull carts. We walked faster and soon broke into a trot as mosquitoes stung our ears, faces, necks, arms, and legs. I even had mosquito bites on my eyelids.

We abandoned all thoughts of claiming our tee shots and dashed the remainder of the par five ninth hole as though we were being chased by wolves. I couldn't unstrap the bags, fold the carts, and toss them into the car trunk fast enough.

"Wow!" we exclaimed as we slammed the car doors shut. "Did that just happen?"

Thinking positively, however, the mosquito attack enabled us to shave five or six strokes off our final score.

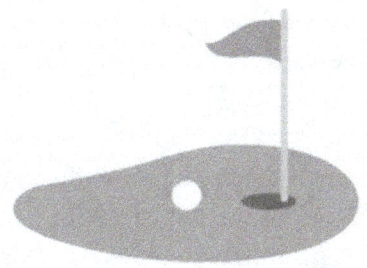

CHAPTER 38

And then she told me . . .

Remember your elementary school days, long before we became convinced we knew all there is to know, when whatever the teacher said had to be true because, well, she said so?

Yes, I said "she," not to be stereotyping but because all of my elementary school teachers were women. Certainly, not all of the world's teachers are female, so while we might be conditioned to think of first- through sixth-grade teachers as women, we also don't expect anybody other than men to be instructors in certain other areas. It is the way we grew up.

One of those certain other areas might be golf. Think about your own experience. A friend tells you he's had a golf lesson. Does your mind's eye see a man teaching?

• • •

Paige Cavalier stepped up to the tee pad and lined up thirty or so yellow range balls. Poised and practiced, she was ready to watch, analyze, and teach her latest student: me.

The assistant pro at my Naples club, Glen Eagle, Paige works with head golf professional Lucas Muzzey on all of the services club golfers expect, from lessons to league and tournament operations to rules interpretations and pro shop staff supervision. I had had a helpful lesson a year prior from Lucas, but a year is plenty long enough for new bad habits to hinder my swing, so I scheduled a refresher with Paige.

She is the seventh pro to provide me with instruction. That's not a lot of people over the span of five decades of golf, but consider that for my first twenty years in the game I didn't know enough to know I was bad. I had no inclination to pay hard-earned money to have somebody tell me how to improve my game.

Then, there's always the fact that for most common golfers, we believe deep down in our souls that we can work our way out of a funk. If you take all that into account, it's probably reasonable that I've had seven golf lessons since the time I started to take golf seriously.

None of the previous lessons was taught by a woman. So I entered the practice facility ready but unsure what I should expect. Does that make sense? I'm a firm believer that women can and should do whatever they aspire to do. I do not judge by gender, skin color, or any of the other stuff that society uses to categorize people. I'm not saying I'm perfectly objective, but I do make it a point to try to avoid judging a book by its cover. Nevertheless, I walked to the tee box with a little bit of a man thing twisting in the back of my brain. Can a girl fix a guy's swing?

• • •

My lesson was scheduled in the club's simulator room. Recently installed, the simulator is state of the art, featuring bells and whistles that see everything and spit out data that tell the teacher just how bad her student really is. I'd specified that I was seeking help with my irons, so Paige pulled the 7-iron from my bag and directed me to hit a few for her initial look-see.

The early returns were encouraging. Or so Paige said. But then again, she no doubt knows confident students learn better and appreciates that it's difficult to build confidence if you leave the impression we are in for a long, uphill battle.

She showed me a video that revealed a few flaws with my arms and hips. She explained my left arm bent around the moment of impact, resulting in a tendency to pull shots. The fix, of course, is to lock the left elbow so I get full extension during the swing and follow-through.

Then she told me another no-no was my tendency sometimes to lean to my right on takeaway, forcing my body to sway back left to return to the impact position. Should be simple to fix that, right? Just remind myself, "Don't sway." If I forget, will you please remind me? Perhaps I will write it on the toes of my shoes.

Paige is a veteran of the golf lesson grind. She appears to enjoy herself as she watches, talks, and demonstrates. But it's her job, so though she has an infectious smile and patient demeanor, I'm pretty certain she has days when she wonders why she didn't become an accountant.

I noticed six patches in the drywall to the right of the simulator screen. They were freshly patched, still needing sanding and painting.

"What's up with those?" I asked.

"Shanks," she said. Her student Rick, whose last name I won't reveal, had a rough stretch in his recent lesson.

As I soaked in her teachings, I thought back to my elementary school days. It occurred to me then that Paige was much like the women who taught me reading, writing, and arithmetic. They and Paige too knew I would get it if I applied myself.

Remember I noted earlier that I was unsure what to expect from my lesson with Paige? No worries! I got knowledge, wisdom, sincerity, analysis, instruction, confidence, technique, and a whole lot more. I also learned this ol' dog can still learn a few tricks.

Thank you, Paige Cavalier. You did good.

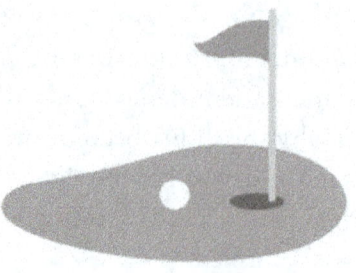

CHAPTER 39

Mark your balls and stay out of my line

One of the things that drives me crazy is people who drive with dogs on their laps. In what reality, I ask myself, does one think it is okay to get into an automobile, beckon your little fluff ball to jump up between your chest and the steering wheel, then shift into gear and motor down the highway?

That is begging for an accident—a calamity that could have very easily been avoided.

So it goes with golf. Many of the mishaps we experience could have easily been avoided. A simple precaution can prevent strokes—and a little courtesy can go a long way to avoid hard feelings.

Consider the simple act of marking your golf balls.

One day around thirty-five years ago, I added an important tool to my golf bag, and I've never gone to the golf course without it since.

The tool is a Sharpie pen. It is essential to fair play, as the means to mark the golfer's ball to make it readily identifiable during the course of play. Yet I marvel at the number of golfers I know who fail to mark their balls. You don't need a Sharpie to do the job, but it certainly is a convenient method.

Inadequately identified balls are just one of the things that bug me. We who golf regularly all have lists. Slow play. Errant shots. Loud noises. Rules ignoramuses. Poor etiquette. And much more. We could fill a book with essays about annoyances, distractions, and infractions.

One of the easiest fixes of course is to mark your golf ball so it can be identified when it's not in your hand or your pocket. Another is to simply avoid tromping on the line of the putts your group will be trying to make.

I played "fun" golf for many years before I ever joined a league or entered a team competition. I was pretty naive about the rules and the do's and don'ts that have accumulated over the span of several hundred years. Some of them are written in the rules book; others are part of the unwritten but widely acknowledged courtesies.

It almost seems like I'm being reckless if I pull from my pocket a ball that does not have two dimples under the number on the ball filled in with black Sharpie ink. I somehow feel more equipped with those ID marks than if I put an unmarked ball in play.

The purpose of marking balls of course is to distinguish them from the gazillion other Titleists, Bridgestones, Callaways, TaylorMades, and whatevers in play and in the woods. If your ball is marked, you run little risk of incurring a penalty for hitting the wrong golf ball just because it looked exactly like the Bridgestone e6 you hit off the tee. One e6 looks pretty much like every other e6, but if your dots, shamrocks, flags, initials, circles, squares, and other telltale markings are visible, you are okay.

Sounds simple, but I'm flabbergasted that many of my friends do not make an effort to mark their balls. It's not like they lose them so quickly that they cannot keep their bag stocked with marked balls. So we play out the often-heard dialogue.

"What are you playing?"

"Titleist 2."

Yeah, okay, like there aren't thousands of them bounding down fairways, ricocheting off trees, and plunking into ponds every day across the land.

Mark 'em, people, and eliminate another bit of doubt from your game.

It's easy to get distracted out there. Who needs another worry? Our minds work overtime out there, often creating mountain-out-of-molehill distractions.

I'm not exactly a fussbudget, but I admit that a little thing that many golfers ignore drives me up the wall. If you walk on my line, I will see it, judge it to be inconsiderate, and allow my brain to dwell on the transgression.

So is it a transgression? No, according to the rules of golf. Nowhere do the rules stipulate that a player cannot walk across the putting line of another player. But sometime during the development of the modern game, golfers began the practice of stepping over or around the line of other players' putts. Thus we have the unwritten point of etiquette relating to keeping one's feet off the grass through which another player is about to roll a ball.

I learned about this bit of courtesy many years ago. I don't recall when or where or even who brought it to my attention, but it has stayed in my head ever since. It's reinforced every time I watch a televised golf tournament and observe the pros walking carefully to avoid tromping where putts might roll.

And yet, despite the obvious care shown by pro golfers, we common golfers walk wherever we damn well please on the greens. It's baffling to me. Yes, putts worth millions of dollars are a lot more important than the putts we make in a league match, but if we can avoid adding deflection into the mix of grain, speed, and gravity, that's a good thing.

I believe golfers fall into three categories on the matter of walking across putting lines: those who do not know any better, those who think

Knowing proper etiquette can keep the peace. The scene is the eighteenth green at Pinehurst Number 2.

it doesn't matter, and we who clench their teeth when a player walks on our line.

"I never knew that rule," said a golfer in response to my mentioning this.

"People have been walking around this green for three hours already this morning, so my steps aren't doing any more harm," said more than one golfer.

"Do you really think the heel on your size twelve FootJoy isn't making a dent under the three hundred pounds you just pressed into the green?" said I when a large friend stepped on rather than over my putting line. Fortunately, he didn't take offense.

A recent "Etiquetteist" column in *Golf* magazine addressed the topic.

"When you shake hands with your playing partners on the first tee, you're making an unspoken agreement to abide by a few basic rules, like not jangling coins in their backswing, not narrating every shot you strike, and not trampling on the ground where they're about to roll a ball," wrote author Josh Sens in the August 18, 2022, *Golf* article.

That's good advice.

So by all means, count all of your strokes, remember to mark your balls and stay out of my line, and we'll get along just fine out there.

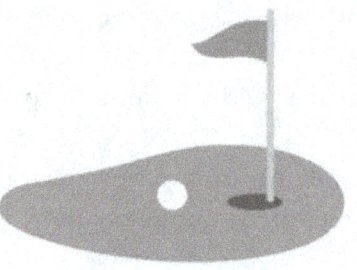

CHAPTER 40

Stupid things I've seen and done

Golfers have a stupid perspective about lightning. There, I said it.

The truth is if you hear thunder or see lightning, you risk getting struck. But golfers have noodled up many beliefs about atmospheric electricity, many of them absolutely false. No less an authority than the National Weather Service advises that if you see lightning, and the thunder arrives within thirty seconds, the storm is close enough to be dangerous. Period.

Many golf courses install lightning detection systems. Some also have systems that not only detect lighting, but also predict it. People should always heed lightning alarms. Amazingly, however, golfers often ignore the alarms. I have. How stupid is that?

If you golf anywhere the weather is warm, you no doubt have seen lightning and heard thunder many times while on the course. Inevitably, somebody in the foursome declares "It's too far away" or "It's going to pass north of us" or some other misguided advice intended to soothe nerves and encourage us to play on. Nobody wants to break up the party.

Never mind that when golf tournament organizers detect lightning, they immediately suspend play, whisk their players to safety, and advise the galleries to seek shelter. In other outdoor sporting events, football and baseball included, play is suspended when lightning is in the vicinity.

The National Weather Service says lightning kills around one thousand people in the US each year. Florida leads the US in lightning deaths. A fair number of them, I would guess, happen because somebody declared "It's still far from us."

That's stupid. But it's not the only stupid thing that happens out there.

I have witnessed numerous ball strikes, many of them completely avoidable. Parking a cart anywhere in front of a player about to hit a golf ball, even at the seemingly most extreme angle, is never a good idea. It's stupid, in fact, but many of us are guilty of standing in the line of fire.

Stupid isn't always dangerous. We all are prone to the occasional stupid utterance, whether at home, on the job, or out on the golf course.

I could have easily kept my mouth shut that morning when I said to one of my friends as he settled over a critical three-foot putt, "Get it close."

I'm not "that guy," but I nevertheless succumbed to the temptation to jab the needle. That was stupid. I regretted it, but the words did come out. Fortunately, the fellow did drain the putt.

Who hasn't attempted an ill-advised shot only to regret it the moment the ball left the clubface? When confronted with a nearly impossible situation, we common golfers are inclined to swing for the hero shot. The wiser choice, most of the time, is to hit the ball out of the trouble or out to a distance where the odds of the next shot hitting the putting surface are pretty good.

I try to follow a friend's advice—the first thing to do when you get in trouble is get out of trouble—but an inner voice often heckles me into trying a very difficult shot. The outcome of most of those desperate attempts often is worse than the original predicament.

Some of our stupid tricks can be dangerous.

Many years ago, during the era of the three-wheel, tiller-steer golf carts, the newspaper where I worked asked another editor and me to represent it at the annual chamber of commerce golf outing. It was my first-ever business golf event, and I dressed for the occasion in my canary-yellow pants and equally loud shirt—high style back in those days.

My fellow editor friend Mike was at the wheel of our cart when, somewhere midround, he decided to play dodge 'em with a squirrel scampering across the fairway. As the rodent darted left and right, Mike, always the fun seeker, tillered left and right. His final left turn missed the furry critter, but the tire dug into the soft dirt, and the back wheels lost traction, putting the three-wheeler into a half spin that pitched me cleanly off my seat to skid along the fairway on my shins.

Luckily our stupid prank didn't cause injury (the squirrel was just fine), but my yellow pants were stained dark green from ankle to knee, and I had a lot of explaining to do back in the clubhouse at dinner that evening.

Golfers everywhere do stupid things. I've seen people reach into an animal hole for a golf ball, poke sticks at hornets' nests, and walk too close to "sleeping" alligators. I once drove too fast on a wet cart path that switchbacked down a steep grade from tee to fairway and nearly spun off into a ravine. Then there was the time an irascible man in my foursome, PO'd that his cart had shut down when he drove too close to the green, slammed the lever into reverse and hurtled full speed backward into an immovable palm tree trunk. He could have been seriously injured.

Golf has a way of inspiring players to think outside the box. As we've noted here, the inspirations aren't always for the best. Next time you are on the golf course, pay attention to what's happening. You will no doubt observe some very creative behavior, some unusual outcomes, and some experiences that will sound pretty amazing back in the grill room after the round is done and the drinks are poured.

Dave Tenaglia knows the rule: the first
thing to do when you're in trouble is
get out of trouble.

CHAPTER 41

Rules are made . . . for everybody

We have the official Rules of Golf and then the rules as misinterpreted by millions of people. Sadly, the gulf between them is as wide as the ocean.

Consider the simple rule about balls coming to rest out-of-bounds and the white stakes that identify OB areas.

I saw this play out recently. True story. Two golfers searched the rough near white out-of-bounds stakes. One found the other's ball nestled in tall grass. The finder called to his buddy.

"Here you are. You're in according to this stake and out according to that one. Your call."

What?

I am not writing today to educate readers about the rights and wrongs regarding golfing situations. But I am prepared to declare that besides the fact the judgment of the fellow offering his ruling was wrong, he also described an impossible situation. OB is determined by the ball's location relative to the straight line between two markers, not some imaginary vector shooting off in a random favorable or unfavorable direction.

"Imaginary" is a keyword in golfers' interpretation (and misinterpretation) of the rules. We all have heard some truly imaginative, but totally fictitious, calls.

White stakes, according to some golfers, are merely suggestions. If the stake is in the way, they move them, even though the rules clearly state that a white stake is not to be moved, even if it impedes the golfer's ability to advance the ball.

Whether you are a PGA Tour winner, your club champion, or a twenty handicapper in your Monday golf league, you are familiar with the term "winter rules." Some courses and clubs adopt winter rules when weather and turf conditions interfere with fair lies. Winter rules permit the golfer to lift and clean their ball and place it favorably no more than six inches from its original location and no closer to the hole. Often, but not always, winter rules apply only in the fairway of the hole being played.

From there, however, comes the temptation to expand the rules to accommodate any number of circumstances. Once you alter the rules, bending or breaking them to satisfy conditions, where does one draw the line in making more adjustments?

Six inches becomes a grip length, which extends to a club length and out beyond to the hypotenuse of a right triangle created by a driver, 5-iron, and putter. Is the ball behind a tree? Kick it out of there. That tree should have been cut down years ago. Is the grass too long where your ball settled down? Fluff it up. The mower probably missed that spot.

The rule is out-of-bounds is marked by white stakes, yet some would declare their ball in bounds if it's resting in short grass.

I once played with a man who declared he was taking no penalty for the ball he lost in the woods because, and I quote him directly, "It's enough of a penalty that I lost a perfectly good golf ball."

Okay. Here's another crazy rules thing.

Sometimes a player in my foursome discovers he's hit the wrong ball. Someone in the group invariably says, "That's okay, just go back and hit your ball. No penalty." And then the guy wins a skin. That's petty larceny.

Bend the rule once and folks shrug. Bend it repeatedly and things can get dicey. Consider the matter of gimme putts.

First, 99.3 percent of golfers have no concept of the fact that there is no such thing as a gimme in stroke play. Explain to them that we cannot speak for the entire field as they beg, "Is that good?" All the others in front and behind us wouldn't necessarily agree that the ball is in the circle of friendship.

Gimmes, nevertheless, are firmly established in golf culture, if not the rules. So what's a gimme? The aforementioned circle of friendship could have as many diameters as the number of players in the game. So the matter also gets murky when it comes down to equal interpretation.

"Gimme" actually describes a first-person action. It's about "me." Give me the putt. The actual act of picking up a ball and stopping the counting of strokes commences when the putt is conceded. A concession is a second-person action, initiated by "you." Concessions are okay in match play, and thus the golf-rules illiterate have interpreted that as okay in whatever game is the play of the day.

A friend recently hit a tree branch with her swing and declared the shot didn't count because the branch provided interference. A friend of my wife stated boldly that she was not counting shots she didn't like.

And so it goes.

All of this, and so much more, are why the rules are published in book form. Many golfers carry the rules in their golf bags. This is not to say we read the books, but it is comforting to know they are there anyway.

CHAPTER 42

Alligators, snakes, and double bogeys

Two New England couples were enjoying a fine round of golf when one of the players asked her husband where she might aim her next shot.

"See that dog out there? Aim for him," Dave said.

But it wasn't a dog.

My friend Jimmy Duggan chuckled as he shared details about that golf day several years ago with his wife, Linda, and friends Judy and Dave Tenaglia on a hilly course in the New Hampshire woods. "It wasn't a dog at all. It was a bear!"

You never know what you might encounter out there.

Wild animals don't obey "golfers only" signs. They have no out-of-bounds. No thicket is too dense nor pond too deep to prevent them from going where they please. They can leap high fences and scamper and slither under them. They can ford the ditches, sun themselves on water hazard banks, and waddle onto greens and tee boxes, and nobody can stop them. They can, it turns out, also fly full speed through the passenger's side of a moving golf cart.

Golf friend Debbie Scorpio had her pregame routine rudely interrupted recently when a low-flying Muscovy duck flew into her side of a golf cart headed to the first tee. Homely waterfowl, Muscovy ducks may very well be the inspiration for the ugly duckling fairy tale. They also are fairly heavy birds.

Debbie was in the wrong place at the wrong time as the ten-pound duck glided in for a splashdown on the pond near the tee box. The thud was audible one hundred feet away. The impact knocked her sunglasses off her face, but other than suffering rattled nerves, she was okay. The duck was less fortunate. It limped, literally, to the nearby water.

The incident was another reminder that we golfers are merely guests in the habitat of animals that lived there long before our bulldozers, graders, tractors, and mowers converted dunes, plains, forests, and valleys into human playgrounds.

In Florida, where people actually do buy swampland, alligators are common sightings on golf courses. Golfers

Tiburon in Naples offers fair warning of the hazards.

ogle gators, snap photos (guilty!), and generally admire the dinosaur specimens stretching out twelve feet and longer. They may appear to be docile—sleeping even—but golfers are regularly reminded the beasts are capable of bursts of speed. No prey is too much for a hungry alligator. Venture too close and you are certainly in harm's way.

Snakes are nature's reminder that Satan can mess with our game. I've witnessed cottonmouth water moccasins gliding rectilinearly across fairways, always giving the venomous vipers a wide berth. Nonvenomous black racers creep me out, too, but I understand they are important players in golf courses' ecosystems.

The course where I play frequently in Florida is home to several other snake species as well, including pygmy and eastern diamondback rattlers. Golfers strolling into cypress groves or poking through palmetto thickets might encounter one at any time.

I play often in Ohio and Pennsylvania, where bear sightings are on the increase. Several golfers have reported encounters with bear cubs near Youngstown. In Florida, friends Jim and Joyce MacDonald showed quick reflexes as they snapped a cell phone photograph of a black bear loping across the first fairway of their home course.

Sometimes, of course, wild animals pose a more immediate danger.

147

Wild animals, including big gators and venomous snakes, know no out of bounds on golf courses.

Barb and I spied a raccoon one midafternoon on a hot summer day. The animal was in obvious distress. It rolled on the ground and walked in tight circles; foam was visible around the raccoon's muzzle. A busy golf course is no place for a rabid raccoon, so Barb phoned the pro shop. Soon a worker drove out from the maintenance shed and triggered a mercy shot.

Deer love golf courses as much as golfers love them. It's interesting to watch them in the various seasons. Spring is the time to see does and fawns, often twins, walking the meadows around parkland courses. As summer brings lush rough, the deer often wander out to graze on the tender grasses. Come autumn, we see bucks with admirable antlers stalking the does with love on their agenda.

Golf course names don't necessarily promise views of their namesake wildlife. I've never seen a deer at Deer Creek or a buck at Buck Run, a beaver at Beaver Creek Meadows or a fox at Fox Run or the Foxfires in Pinehurst, North Carolina, and Naples, Florida. The only diamondback I saw at Diamondback was a taxidermist's rendition behind glass in the pro shop. On the other hand, I've seen lots of eagles at Glen Eagle, but nary a one at Eagle Sticks.

More and more, golf courses are working toward being more friendly to the animals that live on them. Many today leave unmowed areas between fairways and tee boxes to enable wildflowers to thrive for the birds and the bees and to provide cover for ground-dwelling mammals and reptiles. Turtles, ducks, herons, and egrets live and feed near the ball-eating water hazards.

They all are welcome to share our courses, but Canada geese seem to be taking advantage of the situation. Many golf courses with too much goose poop work hard to shoo the honkers, some even turning dogs out to flush the flocks.

I suppose, however, there is no cure for crows. Smarter than many golfers, the big black birds have adapted quite well to profit from the humans who play in their territory. They wait until we golfers are away from our carts, then glide in to pillage and plunder. I know of watches that have been stolen because crows love shiny stuff, and even though I know I should hide my snack crackers, I have lost a few too many packs to hungry crows. "I hope you choke on them!" I holler at birds flying off with the snack I was hoping to enjoy at the turn.

Such is life. We always hold hope that our next shot will be great, we'll catch glimpses of wildlife, we will avoid collecting goose droppings in the grooves of our shoes, and we'll enjoy our crackers before the crows find them.

CHAPTER 43

My favorite golf course

A parcel of land covering 144 acres in southern Mahoning County, Ohio, is the location of a curious crossroads. The intersection there figuratively connects Native Americans, colonial Connecticut business venturers, coal and limestone mining, and veterans of the Revolutionary and Vietnam wars.

Long before the colonies won independence after the Revolutionary War, Native American cultures claimed the lands that today are the counties of Northeast Ohio. As many as twelve thousand years ago, indigenous people lived off the land of Mahoning County, Ohio, and hunted mastodons, bears, and other game. They settled into longhouse communities and farmed and traded. By the 1700s, the inhabitants were of the Seneca, Delaware, Shawnee, and Wyandot nations.

Around 1796, they were joined by people of European descent, many of them arriving with bounty land warrants issued for their service in General George Washington's Continental Army. Their new home was the Connecticut Western Reserve, a strip of land across northern Ohio acquired by investors from Suffield, Connecticut. They formed the Connecticut Land Company and promoted their territory as a future home for war veterans.

History can be so darned coincidental. I don't know for sure, but it could very well be that the man who had the brainstorm we know today as Reserve Run Golf Course was a direct descendent of Scottish people arriving with the early settlers of the Connecticut Western Reserve. That there were MacDonalds among those settlers is a pretty good bet.

By 1986, Scotty MacDonald was bound and determined to turn his 144 acres south of Western Reserve Road in Mahoning County into a golf driving range and then eventually into a golf course. The problem, people told him, was nothing much would grow on the ground churned up by coal and limestone strip-mining. The shale and clay surface soil looked more like a Martian landscape than the verdant lands where golf courses grow.

Scotty wouldn't take no for an answer. He recruited partners, including current owner Rick Vernal, and took advantage of good topsoil made available during nearby commercial and highway construction.

In a video recollection of the beginnings of Reserve Run, Scotty tells of the trials and tribulations. "They thought we were nuts." he said, "We had no topsoil."

Not a problem. Scotty recalled the toils associated with trucking six to seven loads of topsoil per hour over the span of ninety-two days to spread across the layout of eighteen fairways and greens. The trucks and drivers were provided by Vernal, founder and owner of RT Vernal Paving and Excavating. Vernal put his graders to work, and Reserve Run went from brown to green over the next couple of years.

It has matured well over nearly four decades and today it is my favorite golf course. It is popular too with visiting golfers who gladly travel an hour or two from the Pittsburgh area to play affordably on a premium course.

Reserve Run is an interesting layout. Not long by most par-seventy standards, the course winds along the shore of a deep, clear lake that was once the pit of a strip mine. It includes mounds, slopes, and doglegs, large putting surfaces, and a finishing hole that rises steeply from the eighteenth fairway. On arrival at the last green, the golfers can look back over the vista of the sixteenth, seventeenth, and eighteenth holes as well as the road from the street to the clubhouse and the adjacent first hole fairway.

Scotty built six par three and four par fives. Bunker-protected greens require quality approach shots for all eighteen holes.

He loved talking to curiosity seekers who stopped at Reserve Run to hit balls on the range before the course was built. One of the early visitors was my wife, Barb. She asked Scotty whether his new golf course would be friendly for women. He replied, "Of course! A woman's money is just as green as a man's."

Scotty is gone now, following a long battle with the aftereffects of his Vietnam War Army service. He was as proud of his Army service as his golf course and, for that matter, his years of teaching in Youngstown City Schools and serving as president of the teachers' union.

Many would describe him as a curmudgeon. Scotty could be irascible one moment and laughing the next. He welcomed buses loaded with visiting golfers and barked at those who showed up late for tee times. He might harangue you one day and greet you like a long-lost Army buddy the next. It is said he and his business partners didn't always see eye to eye.

"Curmudgeon," I suppose, is a term well deserved. But he could own it because Reserve Run was his baby. He was there when the bulldozers, the brush hogs, and the mowers brought to life a veteran's ambitious vision of a premium golf course. He was there for the dumping of truckloads of topsoil and oversaw all of the construction. I never asked him whether he had considered the history of his property. But I find it intriguing that it is built on the boundary of the land reserved for the veterans who fought for America's independence.

All things considered, Reserve Run is a fun place to play. I always look forward to days when Reserve Run is on the schedule of my grasshoppers group. If I were to be relegated to playing just one golf course for the rest of my days, I would make it Scotty's course.

In his last days, Scotty mellowed a bit. He could be found sitting at a table in the pro shop, his laptop open to God-only-knows-what content, and always willing to greet a customer with a smile and a quip.

I never told him how much I enjoyed his course. But if I had mentioned it, I'm sure he would have smiled and told me that's exactly the reason he built it.

A man's dream often is more than merely gaining his own satisfaction. Indeed, dreams are often about being able to bring satisfaction to others.

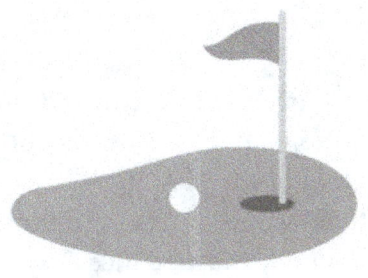

CHAPTER 44

My fantasy foursome

The title of this chapter suggests I have in mind three people with whom I would choose to play a round of golf in the most splendiferous manner.

If only it were that easy.

Think fast! Who would be your fantasy foursome? The answer is not as easy as you think, right?

My friend Leo related a story recently that got me thinking about the possibility I might be invited to play golf with a fantasy foursome. Leo's story was a real-life encounter, so enchanting and charming (and true) that it made me realize how close we might come to actually teeing it up with some most extraordinary people.

I'll tell you more about Leo's story in a few minutes, but first I think it would be good to set the stage.

A fantasy foursome should play their round at a great golf course. I have seen many and played several and could justify selecting any of them. Pebble Beach and Spyglass come to mind. Firestone Country Club is another. Oakmont would be fun. Augusta National is certainly a candidate, as is Donald Ross's Pinehurst Number 2. Any of the dozen or so high-end country clubs I've played would qualify, as would my local muni and the club where I play my snowbird winters in Naples, Florida.

But the venue, I believe, must have history and a place to celebrate when the round is done. So let's enter the lottery for a tee time at St. Andrews (perhaps my VIP guests can pull some strings) and choose from one of the thirty or more pubs in the town on Scotland's Firth of Forth.

Now for the people who will join me. We have no shortage of candidates. The list of possibilities is long. The criteria? It's all up to me. Should they be famous? Yes. Interesting? Certainly. Golfers? Not necessarily. Nice folks? Absolutely. Alive? Maybe, but since this is fantasy, I'm permitted to go back in history.

So I'm looking for a famous and interesting person who isn't necessarily a pro golfer but who absolutely must be nice.

At this point, you are wondering whether this fantasy thing is just a pipedream. Hey, it could happen. Work with me.

When I was a Little Leaguer, my active imagination allowed me to see a day when Rocky Colavito would beckon me from the dugout at Cleveland Municipal Stadium to take a few swings during batting practice. Why not? It was, after all, only batting practice.

Many trips around the sun later, my imagination is still vivid. It could happen someday that three interesting people might send me a text message inviting me to join them on the first tee at St. Andrews and for a pint or two of Belhaven at The Dunvegan.

What constitutes famous and interesting? They would have to have done something significant, and they don't spend every day bragging about it. I've played golf with a Hall of Famer (one hole anyway), met some baseball and football players, and even shaken hands with two US presidents. So any of them would be cool in a fantasy foursome.

So now let's return to Leo's story. He'd been invited to play with a member of Latrobe Country Club. As fate would have it, they were scheduled to follow a particular foursome, which included the owner of the golf course, Arnold Palmer.

Leo and his pals watched as Palmer teed up his ball, aimed down the first fairway, and hit a sweeping slice that landed in the trees. Without hesitation, he reached in his pocket for another ball, teed it up, and took another mighty swing that also cut right into the woods. Palmer called for another ball, put it on the tee, and struck a perfect shot that landed in the middle of the fairway.

He turned to Leo and his friends, grinned, and offered great advice: "Hit 'em 'til you're happy, boys. Hit 'em 'til you're happy!"

So I'm putting Arnold Palmer in my fantasy foursome.

Joining us will be LPGA Hall of Famer Kathy Whitworth. I had an opportunity to play a hole with her in a fundraiser at Glenmoor Country Club in Canton, Ohio, many years ago. One of the side competitions during that memorable day was a "beat the pro" hole. The challenge was laid out on a par three. Any player who put his or her shot inside Kathy's won a brand-new driver. She won eighty-eight times on the LPGA Tour, more than any pro golfer in history, but I beat her that day. I still own her driver and will bring it to St. Andrews for our fantasy round.

So it's Arnold, Kathy, and me. We need another player.

I hope he's not busy that day. I would be honored to tee it up with former President Barack Obama. He is a Nobel Peace Prize winner, unflappable, loves golf, and just seems to be a pretty cool guy.

Palmer, Whitworth, Obama, and me. I'm sure we'll have a blast. I will let you know how it goes.

CHAPTER 45

Feed it, water it, love it

If you want to get Lane Price going, ask him about growing grass.

A sturdy man with an easy smile, Lane sat comfortably in his air-conditioned office as the sun beat down outside on the golf course where he is superintendent. The AC provided comfort, but outside it was hot, and the sun was pulling precious moisture from the soil and evaporating water from the ponds that are the lifeblood for Lane's fairways and greens.

It goes without saying that grass is vital to a golf course. It's also true that Lane is vital to his grass.

He forgot for a moment about his day-to-day worries about water, wear, and disease and settled back in his chair to think for a moment before answering my question: why did he get into the business of growing grass for golf courses and maintaining durable, high-quality, disease-resistant playing surfaces? His thick arms folded like stovepipes across his broad chest, he squinted his eyes and leaned forward to speak.

"I told Dad I wanted to go to school to grow grass, and he said, 'What?!' Dad was a banker, and it was hard for him to understand my idea of a career," Lane said in explaining why he pursued a bachelor's degree in turf grass science at the University of Florida's School of Agriculture.

"I'm a farmer in some ways, but we don't harvest the same. We manage differently because our outcome has to fit our situation. It's all so interesting. It takes tools, aerification, water regulation, fertility, soil science. So over a period of time, I convinced Dad that I wanted a different education and needed knowledge about soil chemistry, hydrology, herbicides, pesticides, plant physiology, so many things. And at the end of the day, there's an art that goes into it."

Lane today is the superintendent at Glen Eagle Golf & Country Club in Naples, Florida. He grew up just north of the Southwest Florida city and went off to Gainesville to gain the education and insights that have made him very successful in the art and science of sports turf management. He has earned the highest respect of his colleagues and, more importantly, the people who play on his golf courses.

I say "his" golf courses. Lane projects a love for his turf that is deeper than simply the enjoyment of growing plants. Like the gardener who prizes every plant in his plot, Lane truly is passionate about the eighteen holes winding around more than one thousand homes in Glen Eagle. His affection is personal, and he explains his relationship with turf in human terms.

"I try to get people to understand that it's not going to last forever. Grass is like people. It starts with infancy, newly sprigged grass. It grows to become a strong teen and twenty-year-old, about as tough as it's ever going to be. Then eventually it peaks and starts to just sustain itself for a period of five to seven years; then eventually it gets to a point where it breaks down to where anything—cart traffic, disease, other detrimental factors—injures it and it cannot recuperate. That signals the end of the grass's life cycle, and it needs to be replaced."

Like his colleagues in other sports, Lane faces a plethora of problems. "We have challenges on any kind of sports field, whether it's football, soccer, baseball, whatever. Players put stresses on the grass. Here at Glen Eagle, we put forty thousand rounds of cart traffic on the course every year, and it's a condensed forty thousand on top of that. We beat the turf up with an implement [golf club] and create ball marks when we hit the green. Those are injuries to the living plants. So the way we approach turf maintenance is intense in labor, and it's economically challenging."

A veteran of the turf wars, Lane has gained knowledge and confidence that translates into expertise. He can look at his grass and know what needs to be done. He says there is an art in reading the turf, and he relies on no cookie-cutter program. He also must understand the weather and its effects on his turf.

"Education gave me the basis for knowing what needs to be done, and over the years I've learned that the weather is such a determining factor.

Changes dictate changes."

Lane acknowledged that his job is not only turf related. Glen Eagle invests around $2 million every year for Lane to make the golf course great.

"Turf actually is one of the easier parts. We also have to factor in employee management and deal with our members. I've got my boss and my peers and our industry. Plus there's the business side, accounting and such, which is just as important as the agronomics side.

"But it's pretty cool, really, because when I've had enough of the business stuff, I get to go outside and play in the dirt for a while."

Our conversation turned toward what makes him happy.

Lane paused, looked to the windows of his office, and found the words.

"It's setting up the field of play. It's creating a course for the enjoyment and satisfaction of other people. I tried the landscaping business. I've tried sales. I tried a few other avenues related to the turf industry, but I always am drawn back to the fact that we go out every day and set up a course of play for the enjoyment of a group of people."

Lane Price keeps Glen Eagle in tip-top condition even as forty thousand rounds beat up his turf.

He smiled, his satisfaction coming through on his face as clearly as the words that came from his mouth.

His career has grown from assistant positions to superintendent at other golf clubs around Southwest Florida in various segments of the country club industry—from management companies to single owners to bundled communities. He's accumulated an encyclopedia of turf business experience and the talent to communicate effectively with his constituencies.

"My job includes being able to communicate to the membership about what the needs are and what the outcomes might be. We must let people know why we do what we do and what we need to do it, so when we ask for resources, they know what it is going to do for them. I know I need to create pride in the membership for the product that is here."

He points to his club's annual member-guest, The Talon, as a big opportunity to put a spit-polish shine on his golf course.

"The member-guest is so important to me and our staff. We want to impress our guests, yes, but at the same time, it's great to see our members being proud to bring their guests to the club."

Growing grass. It's more than feeding and watering. It's loving it, and few love their turf as much as Lane Price.

People, equipment, and talent are necessary for excellent playing conditions.

CHAPTER 46

Certain things need not be mentioned

We've covered a lot of topics in this book, but certainly not all there is to know. Golfers' experiences are as broad as life itself. We may talk, worry, and obsess about stuff with our closest friends, but some things just don't need to be spread far and wide.

Consider, for example, the ways in which we handle matters when nature calls. I don't think it needs to be mentioned in this book. I've seen enough emergencies, my own and those of friends, to know that when it's time, it's time. Sometimes your coffee and breakfast burrito don't kick in until the third or fourth hole, when the clubhouse and halfway house are too far for quick relief. Many a nice golf towel has been sacrificed in the line of duty.

Nobody needs to know our dirty laundry, right? I could tell you about the poor fellow whom we encountered in a golf course restroom stall equipped with its own wash basin. The guy was in there a long time, the water running nonstop. I don't need to tell you what he was doing in there.

Nor do we need to discuss the other form of necessary elimination. It's easy in most of our life situations. My boater brother-in-law, Gary, for instance, declares it's time to check the prop and jumps into the lake. "Prop's fine," he declares as he climbs aboard and takes the helm.

For men on the golf course, it's pretty much as easy as Gary's solution. Taking care of number one is no big deal. Everybody knows what's happening when someone in the foursome sneaks behind a tree or ducks into the woods. Some guys don't even bother to hide, opting just to turn their backs to the boys.

But we don't need to dwell on that, even though it's obviously more complicated for women. I'm sure most women have their own tactics when squirming is not going to work much longer. The woods may be the answer, but sometimes there are no trees for hundreds of yards, so strategically parked golf carts provide the necessary cover.

One of the craziest things I don't need to discuss is the uninhibited woman who simply pulled her shorts down and squatted in plain view. I should have looked away, but the scene was too funny, and she obviously couldn't have cared less.

Another unmentionable is torn clothing. Who needs to read about that in a golf book? I could tell you, for instance, about the time my friend bent down to align his ball for an upcoming putt. The seam of his shorts parted like it was cut with shears, the crotch-to-belt rip revealing his tighty-whities. None of us had spare shorts, rain pants, or safety pins, so he shrugged his shoulders and finished the round with his underwear in proud view.

Ninety-eight percent of golfers show up at the course feeling fine, so I don't need to cover the fact that a few folks make it to the first tee with a headache and stomach churning. A night of partying proved to be a bit too much for one fellow who excused himself, turned toward the bushes, and hurled his belly's contents. It was clear he'd eaten pizza along with his beer. Amazingly, he carded a 73 that day.

Did I mention certain things need not be mentioned?

CHAPTER 47

The final round

Actually, this book has no fitting ending. Yet.

All of us, especially you who have stayed with me through the first forty-six essays in *The Common Golfer*, have much still to accomplish. Where our journeys take us is still to be revealed, but onward our journeys go even as we stop along the road, and the fairways and greens, to smell the roses and count our scores.

We forge forward in life and in golf. To quote American poet Robert Frost, "But I have promises to keep/And miles to go before I sleep."

How true.

I choose not to write a hard finish to this book. We all know we will play a final round, and we all hope we haven't already signed our last scorecard. As I have written throughout, golfers are sport's optimists. New opportunities arrive seventy, eighty, ninety times a round and more. Regardless of yesterday's score, we believe the next round could very well be the best we've ever played. So in the meantime, we practice our swings, try new clubs, schedule tee times, ID our balls, and swagger to the first tee with hopes running high.

Even after we walk off the eighteenth green, the game is not done. Tomorrow we will go to the first tee again.

In fact, when we think it through, we invest our entire golfing life in preparing for our next great shot, if not our best round ever. The journey has only one destination, and it is impossible to know it until we arrive.

But of course we are mortal. James Dodson best chronicled the end of a golfing lifetime in his acclaimed book, *Final Rounds: A Father, a Son, the*

Golf Journey of a Lifetime. If you have not read Dodson's book, do it soon.

The rest is up to you. Literally.

I conclude *The Common Golfer* with a simple request to readers: Tell us why you are passionate about golf. What do you love? Who inspired you? What is your best memory?

This book is for and about us common golfers, so your stories are as important to the world's golf chronicle as those in my little book. Please write your chapter of *The Common Golfer* and share it with your family and friends. Feel free to broaden your impact and publish your chapter on my Jack Wollitz Facebook page and post your favorite photos.

You're away. Chapter 48 is for you to write. Go ahead and take your shot. It may very well be your best ever.

The late Joe Colella on the fairway of Number 16 at Kennsington in Ohio.

Acknowledgments

First and foremost, I wish to thank my wife, Barb, with whom I have golfed for a half century. If she's your friend, you are truly blessed. If she's in your golf foursome, hang on! It's going to be a fun day.

I also thank two talented women, Lee-Ann DeMeo and Joyce Watt MacDonald. Lee-Ann is the creative director at ad agency Innis Maggiore. She graciously agreed to design the covers of this book. Her work is always spectacular. Joyce is a dear friend who loves to read. I tapped her enthusiasm for a thorough preview of *The Common Golfer* to determine whether the stories were written in a manner to please readers. Her trained eyes and kind words are most appreciated.

I have so many good golf friends in Ohio, Florida, and elsewhere who, whether they remember or not, endured my idiosyncrasies, challenged my game, or otherwise got inside my head to inspire the essays in this book. I do wish to specifically acknowledge Stan Czech, Jim Zarlenga, Ralph Roberts, Jack Savage, Mike Malito, Cosmo Pecchia, George Spencer, Rich Herman, Bucky Bequeath, John Kushner, Joe Meyers, Rich Getch, Jimmy DeCapita, Ted Suffolk, Jim Halloran, and Paul Pirko, along with the guys in the Holy Family Golf League in Poland, Ohio. I also salute my better ball match play friends at Glen Eagle Golf & Country Club in Naples, Florida: Mike Kreeger, Tim Leary, Dave Tenaglia, Dan Blanch, Glenn Gallant, Dave Newcomb, Bob Brown, Jimmy Duggan, Jim MacDonald, Bob Guido, Paul Parrone, Fred Suman, Don Nicholas, John Horgan, and Mark Ondrako.

Diane Laney Fitzpatrick is a former newspaper colleague and lifelong friend whose own drive to write and publish helped kickstart me and my books. I also wish to thank teacher, journalist, and my former student David Lee Morgan Jr. for introducing me to publishers Scott Ryan and David Bushman.

Thanks too to Innis Maggiore associate Jeff Rios for loaning me his copy of Rick Reilly's *Missing Links*. Reilly's novel planted the first seed from which *The Common Golfer* sprouted.

And finally, I thank my father, Bob Wollitz, for looking the other way when I pilfered his golf clubs to swat balls around the backyard at home. From such a simple backyard pastime sprang a passion to hit a golf ball, find it, and hit it again, believing every single time that the next shot I was about to hit could be the best I've ever struck.

More To Read by Jack Wollitz

Order at TuckerDSPress.com

ABOUT THE AUTHOR

Jack Wollitz is a former newspaper editor and public relations executive. Now retired from the work-a-day world, he continues as a columnist for two Ohio newspapers and as a freelance magazine feature writer. Jack fills his retirement time with fishing trips and three to four rounds of golf each week in Ohio and Florida with friends and family. His experiences on and around golf courses are the feedstock for his new book, *The Common Golfer*, aptly subtitled "Celebrating the Game's Ordinary and Extraordinary People, Places and Things." After sixty years of playing the game, Jack concludes that common golfers like himself, people with an uncommon passion for the game, are true believers that regardless of what has transpired during their round, the next shot they are about to hit may very well be the best they've ever struck. His first book, *The Common Angler*, helped inspire *The Common Golfer*, as they both explore the whys of the respective sports and the optimism and enthusiasm of their participants. Jack and his wife, Barb, reside in Poland, Ohio, and Naples, Fla., and are proud that daughter Betsy and her husband, Dr. Irfan Khan, are continuing the family golf tradition.

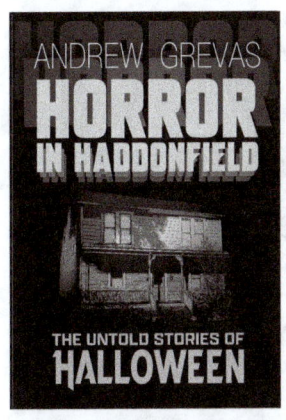